22 DAYS IN NEW ZEALAND

THE ITINERARY PLANNER

BY ARNOLD SCHUCHTER

Library of Congress Catalog No. 87-043129

Published by John Muir Publications
Santa Fe, New Mexico
Printed in U.S.A.

Editor   Richard Harris
Design/Production   Mary Shapiro
Maps   Janice St. Marie
Cover Map   Michael Taylor
Typography   Copygraphics, Inc., Santa Fe, NM

ISBN 0-912528-86-9

CONTENTS

How to Use This Book   5
New Zealand is Unique   19
Itinerary   24
Day 1   Arrive in Auckland   29
Day 2   Around Auckland   37
Day 3   Waitakere Range and North Shore   42
Day 4   Auckland to the Bay of Islands   45
Day 5   Russell—Bay of Islands—Waitangi—Kerikeri   53
Day 6   Bay of Islands—Coromandel Peninsula   58
Day 7   Coromandel Peninsula—Rotorua   61
Day 8   Rotorua—Lake Taupo   66
Day 9   Lake Taupo—Tongariro National Park—Wanganui   73
Day 10   Wanganui—Wellington   78
Day 11   Wellington   82
Day 12   Wellington to Christchurch   85
Day 13   Christchurch Region   90
Day 14   Christchurch—Queenstown   96
Day 15   Queenstown   103
Day 16   Queenstown—Te Anau   107
Day 17   Te Anau—Milford Sound   112
Day 18   Te Anau—Queenstown—Wanaka   115
Day 19   Wanaka to Fox and Franz Josef Glaciers   118
Day 20   Franz Josef—Hokitika—Greymouth   121
Day 21   Greymouth—Arthur's Pass N.P.—Christchurch   125
Day 22   Christchurch—Banks Peninsula   128

22 Days in New Zealand

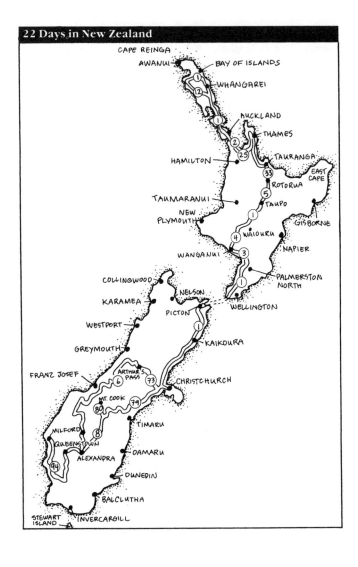

HOW TO USE THIS BOOK

New Zealand's coastlines are fringed with coves, bays, rocky cliffs and headlands, fiords, steep mountains, calm and surf-swept golden and black sand beaches. Volcanic and alpine mountains form the centerpieces of national parks no more than a few hours' drive from either coastline, and in many instances only minutes away. These parks include one out of every 13 acres in the nation, preserved for the benefit of all nature lovers. The South Pacific Ocean on the east and the Tasman Sea on the west unify New Zealand's contrasting coasts on two islands as large and as different from each other as the British Isles or Japan. Sheep also unify the diverse New Zealand landscape—a profusion of 70 million gentle woolly creatures speckling every pasture and hillside, innocently inducing in travelers an uncanny sense of *deja vu* with almost every new roadway.

Following the do-it-yourself tour described in this book, you will:

■ Acclimate to Kiwi country by covering the gamut of urban, coastal, island and mountain "bush" activities in the Auckland region, and enjoy delicious meals.

■ Tour the glorious Bay of Islands and then giant kauri forests on the west coast of historic Northland.

■ Travel south to Wellington passing through scenic Coromandel Peninsula, explore Rotorua-Taupo-Tongariro's volcanic mountains and trout-filled lakes and rivers, and maybe jetboat down the beautiful Wanganui River to the "Garden City" of the same name.

■ Cross Cook Strait on the Inter-Island Ferry from Wellington through the South Island's fabulous Marlborough Sounds.

■ Leave the "sun belt of the South Island" from the ferry port of Picton and head down the Kaikoura Coast to the marvelous variety of attractions in the Christchurch region and the South Island's most picturesque city.

■ Travel from Christchurch over Burke's Pass and past glacial lakes to Mt. Cook National Park.

■ Pass through Mackenzie Country, rimmed by the Southern Alps, over Lindis Pass to the spectacular mountains, lakes and rivers of Queenstown, Te Anau, Fiordland National Park and world renowned Milford Sound.

■ Drive through the beautiful Wanaka/Mt. Aspiring National Park region over Haast Pass to the west coast's Fox and Franz Josef Glaciers.

■ Return to Christchurch over Arthur's Pass after exploring some of the west coast's lakes, as well as greenstone and gold-mining attractions, to complete your tour on beautiful Banks Peninsula.

For each day, this book provides:
1. A **Suggested Schedule** of where to go, in what order, how long to stay there, what to see and how to travel between destinations.
2. The most unique and scenic **Sightseeing Highlights**, rated: ▲▲▲ "Don't miss"; ▲▲ "Try hard to see"; and ▲ "Worthwhile if you can make it."
3. My recommendations for **Where to Eat** and **Where to Stay**, in all budgetary ranges.
4. **Itinerary Options**, activities and side trips, usually requiring more time or money.
5. **Maps** of all areas covered in this tour.

Customize your own itinerary. This guide can be followed literally for 22 days, or you can select any day or combination of days as your itinerary, or even take only one itinerary option in one chapter and make it your entire vacation. Some travelers want to "see it all," while others prefer to concentrate their time in a few selected areas with a large variety of activities or a single, unique sporting/outdoor activity such as deep-sea fishing, diving, white-water rafting, or perhaps just relaxing. Each "Day" in this book is modular and, within certain limitations, can be rearranged to suit your travel style. With the exception of about five days spent in three cities (Auckland, Wellington, and Christchurch), most sightseeing and activities on both islands center on coastlines, mountains, lakes and rivers.

22 Days in New Zealand is for the young at heart who love the outdoors. Seeing the best of New Zealand's diverse landscapes and coastal waters makes for three weeks of very full days. The itinerary guides you step by step through each one of these days to experience a full range of the finest this marvelous country has to offer.

New Zealand's natural beauty needs to be seen on foot (walking, hiking, "tramping," "trekking," climbing, and even golfing), by water transport (rowboat, sailboat or yacht, cruiser, ferry, hydrofoil, catamaran, jetboat, canoe, and raft), by air (light plane, helicopter, pontoon plane, skiplane and balloon), underwater and underground. In addition to miles of interconnected tracks for hiking enthusiasts, I will tell you about routes for short and easy walks in and around cities, other touring bases and scenic spots. Pack your most comfortable pair of walking shoes.

Throughout this book, I describe special-interest sporting activities for those who wish to take advantage of the incomparable opportunities New Zealand presents. Anglers, for example, will have an incredible variety of world-class choices. On the North Island, there's deep-sea and sport fishing in the Bay of Islands, Hauraki Gulf and the Bay of Plenty. New Zealand is one of those rare places where "fish stories" probably are true. Believe everything you've heard about trout fishing in the North Island's Rotorua-Taupo lake system and the Tongariro River and its tributaries; or on the South Island, Lakes Rotoiti and Rotoroa (and dozens of nearby rivers), Hanmer Springs' Hurruni and Waiau Rivers, the Raikaia and Rangitata Rivers south of Christchurch, the legendary Mataura, Oreti and Aparima in the southeast, and sports fishing in Marlborough Sounds.

New Zealand is golfers' heaven. You can spend your entire vacation moving from green to glorious green, with small or no green fees, each setting more beautiful than the last: Auckland's Muriwai, Bay of Island's Waitangi, Rotorua's Arikikapakapa (with boiling mud pool "traps" and hot pool "hazards"), Christchurch's Russley or Shirley, Dunedin's Otago Golf Club, and dozens of others.

Cost and Budget Considerations

The prices quoted in this book for accommodations and meals are for two people traveling together unless otherwise indicated. All prices are in New Zealand dollars, shown as NZ$.

New Zealand is not expensive for an extended vacation, as long as you plan your budget carefully and stick to it. A single person can expect to spend NZ$40-$50 a day for a room, NZ$25-$35 for meals, NZ$60 for daily sightseeing excursions, tours, admission fees, etc., and NZ$10 for entertainment and miscellaneous. A couple will save on the room cost per person but on nothing else—maybe spending a little more on sightseeing and entertainment. Two persons will spend about US$4400 for 22 days, plus US$2000 for international airfare. If you rent a car for 22 days, it will cost at least NZ$75 per day plus gas, for another NZ$1650 (about US$1000). The approximate grand total for 22 days is US$7400 for two persons ($3700 per person). This does not include souvenirs, sheepskin or wool purchases, skiing, cruising or flightseeing.

An individual budget traveler, staying in youth hostels, using a Travelpass, watching pennies for meals and choosing to hike rather than pay for sightseeing excursions, can make the 22-day trip for US$2200 or less, depending on the season.

Entry Requirements

As an American citizen, you need a passport valid for at least three months beyond the date of your expected departure from New Zealand and a return ticket. No visa is required if you plan to stay less than 30 days. No inoculations are required. Each person over 17 can bring in a quart of liquor, wine or beer, 200 cigarettes, 50 cigars, plus up to NZ$250 worth of duty-free items. Bring in as much money as you like, and there is no duty on your other personal possessions. Prohibited items include food, plants, animals or animal products, insects, other squirming objects (except children) and drugs other than over-the-counter and prescriptions.

If you plan to spend at least three weeks in New Zealand, technically you can be asked to prove that you have at least US$1000 with you in cash, travelers checks or valid credit cards. I've never experienced this type of welcoming "investigation" and, chances are, neither will you.

Currency

New Zealand has one, two, five, ten, 20 and 50 dollar notes, and one, two, five, ten, 20, and 50 cent coins. As of this writing a New Zealand dollar is worth US$.65, but the relative value of both dollars changes daily. Though a U.S. dollar buys about 50% more than a New Zealand dollar, you must budget carefully or sleeping, eating and transportation costs will chew up your resources almost as fast as back in the U.S.

Travelers checks can be exchanged for New Zealand currency at any bank without a fee and even earn you a slight premium over exchanging U.S. dollars. Trading banks are open from 9:30 a.m. to 4:00 p.m. Monday through Friday, but not on Saturdays or public holidays. American Express, Bankcard, Diners Club, Mastercard and Visa credit cards are welcomed at large and medium-sized hotels, tourist shops and higher-priced restaurants, but you'll enjoy more flexibility with a supply of both U.S. and New Zealand travelers checks and, off the beaten path, about NZ$100 in cash.

Seasons, Holidays and Hours

New Zealand's seasons are opposite those of the U.S. Spring is September through November; summer, December through February; autumn, March through May; and winter, June through August. The climate is temperate. Seasonal variations are noticeable, but only extreme in the mountains and the far southern part of the South Island. You can gaze at snow on the mountains of both islands from their mild coastlines. Winter on the North Island tends to be wet, but only dismal for a few mid-winter days in Auckland. On the South Island, when wet weather hits the mountains, frequently with fierce winds, watch out for rapidly flooding rivers and streams or blizzards that happen before you can say, "Let's get out of here!"

In July, the coldest month in Auckland, the average temperature is 58 degrees Fahrenheit. July also has the most days of rain (12), so the dampness (70% humidity) can make it seem colder. January, the warmest month in Auckland, is also one of the driest (6 inches rainfall) but still humid (64%). Christchurch, a little colder in mid-winter (51 degrees) and a little cooler in mid-summer (71 degrees), also has high humidity (57-70%).

There are substantial variations throughout each island. It rains twice as much in the Bay of Islands as on the southeast coast south of Gisbourne. Most of the north and east coasts of the South Island are drier than the North Island. The west coast can be quite wet and colder than on the east side of the Southern Alps.

Combine a summer (December to February) trip to New Zealand with a trip to southeastern Australia (Sydney to Adelaide) or Tasmania. If any place in the South Pacific compares to New Zealand for concentrated natural beauty, it is the island of Tasmania. Or plan a winter trip to New Zealand for skiing (July-August) with a visit to Australia's Queensland, Northern Territories or Western Australia during some of their best weather, and perhaps to Victoria and Tasmania for more skiing. John Gottberg's *22 Days in Australia* tells you how to economically explore the other wonders "down under."

Unless you plan to ski or you are en route to the northern half of Australia, don't travel to New Zealand in the winter. Fall and especially spring and summer are more beautiful and drier. But in the summer months, when school is out and New Zealanders are on holiday, accommodations, transportation and tourist attractions are scarce and heavily booked, prices go up and you have to scramble and pay more for less.

National and School Holidays: For travel planning purposes, the significance of New Zealand's national holidays is that the country shuts down. Don't arrive on one or try to travel anywhere. Stay put. Don't drive if you are low on gas. Take a walk, hike, sail or whatever you like, purchasing food the day before. Don't bother looking for restaurants or pubs except maybe a stray milk bar in the hinterlands. Be prepared for these holidays:

New Years Day
Waitangi Day—February 6
Good Friday and Easter Monday
Anzac Day—April 25
Queen's Birthday—first Monday in June
Labour Day—fourth Monday in October
Christmas Day
Boxing Day—December 26

If the holiday falls on a Tuesday through Thursday, it shifts to the previous Monday; on Friday though Sunday to the following Monday. Also watch for local holidays in every part of the country, such as January 29 in Auckland and January 22 in Wellington, which can be equally hazardous to your travel plans.

The main school and family vacation period is from mid-

December to the end of January. Schools are also closed for two weeks in May and in the beginning of August.

Time Zones: The most confusing aspect of the trip to New Zealand is the difference in day, date and time back home. You cross the International Date Line and "lose" a day, gaining it back on your return. Fortunately, New Zealand has just one time zone—12 hours ahead of Greenwich Mean Time. California is a day and four hours later: Monday at noon in Auckland is Tuesday at 4:00 p.m. in Los Angeles or 7:00 p.m. in New York. New Zealand observes Daylight Saving Time, advancing one hour from the last Saturday in October to the first Sunday in March. The easiest way to deal with it is not to think about it.

Don't leave the U.S. on Friday, or you'll arrive in Auckland on Sunday when many of the city's tourist attractions, information centers, and restaurants are closed. Instead, leave on Thursday or Saturday.

Shopping Times and Business Hours: Most stores are open from 9:00 a.m. to 5:30 p.m. Monday to Thursday (until 9:00 p.m. on Friday in major cities) and on Saturday until noon. Only tourist shops in season and dairies will be open Sunday. Offices, businesses and post offices are open weekdays from 8:00 a.m. to 5:00 p.m. Banks are open from 10:00 a.m. to 4:00 p.m. Monday through Friday.

What to Bring

Be prepared for any kind of weather at any time of year with wet weather gear, a windproof jacket, light and heavier sweaters (which can be purchased in New Zealand) and some medium-weight clothing, shorts, a swimsuit, sunglasses and sun screen (expensive in New Zealand), comfortable walking/hiking shoes and good socks. Men who plan to eat out at a splurge restaurant or visit nightclubs should bring an appropriate jacket, shirt and tie. Women, bring a dress or skirt and blouse. And, of course, bring your 35mm camera with plenty of film, which costs less in the U.S.

If you're taking an electric appliance, such as a hair dryer, bring a voltage transformer and a three-pin flat adapter plug with the top two pins set at an angle. New Zealand runs on 230 volts AC, though many hotels and motels provide 110-volt AC sockets.

On trans-Pacific airline flights you are limited to two checked bags per person, so if you have a lot to pack or expect to bring back bulky purchases use the largest suitcases you can find. Pack light, and take no more than two sets of anything.

Flying to New Zealand

Continental Airlines, Air New Zealand, United Airlines and

French Airlines have direct service from the U.S. They all offer essentially the same fares for three seasons: low-season (April 1 to the end of September), US$996 round-trip; shoulder-season (October and November), US$1095; and high-season (December through March), US$1295, with another US$30 for the return from Christchurch. Check with each airline for special promotional fares. Ask specifically about rental car and accommodation packages.

Book your New Zealand flight far enough ahead to take advantage of advanced purchase excursion (APEX) fares. Without a special promotional fare, off-season APEX fares with stopover privileges in two destinations besides New Zealand (Hawaii, Cook Islands or Tahiti) cost about US$1000. Ideally, in order to make travel time adjustments in easy stages, plan to break your journey en route each way in Hawaii, Fiji or Tahiti on a super-fare with stopover privileges. Unless you plan to take advantage of stopover privileges, try to avoid a change of planes in Hawaii or a stop in Tahiti; either poses the risk of delay in the event that the connecting flight to Auckland is late.

Getting Around By Car or Camper Van

Looking at New Zealand on a globe or in an atlas, merely a tiny sliver in the vast South Pacific next to the far larger Australian continent, easily leads to the illusion that North and South Islands can be covered comfortably in a car in a matter of days. Your suspicion that this isn't true will be confirmed quickly. New Zealand has a good network of roads, but they are not freeways. This itinerary is based on an average driving speed of 40 mph or less.

Rental cars normally cost US$60-$85 per day with unlimited mileage. Save money with a discount package that combines car rental, accommodations and APEX airfare. Purchased as a "tour module" from a travel packager such as Continental Newmans Vacations (tel. 213-277-6401), the daily car rental cost drops considerably: US$49 per day for a manual shift Toyota Starlet; US$52 per day for a manual Toyota Corolla; US$68 for an automatic Corolla; and US$70 for a Ford Falcon Sedan. A 10-seater minibus rents for US$73-$77 per day. (Four or more travelers on a tight budget can split the rental of a mini-bus for not much more than the cost of a public transportation travel pass and enjoy more freedom and flexibility.) All tour module rental costs are for seven to 14-day periods and require purchase of Continental Airlines international tickets.

You may want to consider putting a camper-van rental in the package at about the same price and save additional money by staying in caravan parks. Continental Newmans Vacations has excellent 7-day deals on motor homes: two-berth pop-top,

US$330; two-plus-two, US$429; four-berth motor caravan, US$490; and six-berth motor home, US$612. The savings on accommodations are offset by higher gas consumption. Gas (petrol) can cost almost $4 per gallon.

Traffic keeps to the left hand side of the road. Start driving on uncrowded local streets, rather than main highways, to get used to left-hand drive. For the first day, pay very careful attention until left-hand drive becomes comfortable and automatic. Each morning remind yourself about left-hand drive before you start driving.

Immediately learn the "right hand rule": always give way to traffic approaching on your right except for a car directly in front that intends to turn right. The maximum speed limit is 100 kilometers per hour (roughly 60 mph), or 50 kph (30 mph) in built-up areas. An "L.S.Z." (Limited Speed Zone) sign means no speed limit—use your good judgment.

Don't drink when driving! New Zealand laws are even tougher than those in the U.S. Watch out for sheep and cows, school buses and children. Keep your gas tank full, use chains when required, don't try to drive across flooding rivers, and have a safe and enjoyable trip.

By Coach and Train

Hiring a car or camper-van is extremely helpful but not necessary in order to tour New Zealand using this guide.

The New Zealand Railway Road Services (NZRR) provides coach, train and ferry service around the country. There are three **Travelpass** discount packages: eight-day (US$206), 15-day (US$313) and 22-day (US$363) in December-January (high season), and US$177, US$247 and US$305 for eight-, 15- and 22-day passes from February 1 to December 14 (low-season). At these prices, Travelpasses deserve serious consideration for part or all of the 22-day itinerary. Travelpasses must be purchased in the U.S., but their February-to-December (low-season) 15-day or 22-day passes can be purchased in New Zealand. From December 15 to January 31, all three passes have to be purchased in New Zealand. Each pass is undated; starting on the day you begin travel on the NZRR system, use is on a consecutive day basis. Additional days (up to six) can be bought for US$16 per day. Using these passes you can travel anywhere by coach, train and the Inter-island Ferry from Wellington to Picton for less than US$14 (NZ$23) per day, whereas full-day bus travel alone otherwise can cost NZ$20-$50. The Travelpass also provides discounts at Best Western Motels.

Also, ask your travel agent about current prices on seven-day, 10-day and 15-day **Kiwi Coach Passes** jointly offered by NZRR, Mount Cook Line and Newmans Coachlines, which gets you everywhere you want to go for about NZ$15 per day. You must purchase the pass before leaving the U.S.

By Air

Four major carriers—Air New Zealand, Mount Cook Airlines, Newmans Airways and Ansett Airlines (the competitive newcomer)—provide ample air services between all major cities and tourist centers, supplemented by numerous smaller airlines. Purchase a Mt. Cook Lines (Suite 1020, 9841 Airport Blvd., Los Angeles, CA 90045, tel. 213-684-2117) **Kiwi Air Pass** before leaving the U.S. and you can travel once on any sector of their scheduled air routes for 14 days (with reservations) within a 30 day period at a seasonal price of about US$300. The Kiwi Air Pass will enable you to fly between Auckland, Bay of Islands, Rotorua, Christchurch, Mt. Cook, Queenstown and Milford.

An equally attractive alternative is the 14-day or 21-day **Air New Zealand Air Pass**, which entitles you to unlimited stopovers, including backtracking, for about US$342.

Ansett New Zealand flies from Auckland to Christchurch, then to Glentanner Airport (near Mt. Cook), Wanaka, Queenstown, Te Anau and Milford Sound. Ansett only flies to Wellington and Rotorua on the northern route between Christchurch and Auckland. Ansett has two types of discount deals requiring pre-purchase in the U.S. together with an excursion/economy ticket or a frequent flyer membership on any international carrier: **Discover New Zealand**, 20% off regular economy, one-way only; and **See New Zealand**, 30% off round trip fares (with no minimum stays). In New Zealand or the U.S., Ansett has two other discount fares with limited seating: **Goodby 43**, one-way only and no minimum stay—for example, Auckland to Christchurch, costs NZ$115 (the regular fare is NZ$199)—and **Goodby 35**, round-trip with a two night minimum.

Where to Stay

New Zealand offers an outstanding variety of accommodations at reasonable prices, especially for U.S. (as well as European or Japanese) currency. Carry cash or travelers checks and don't depend on credit cards unless you're following the hotel/motel chain circuit. You can wait until you arrive in New Zealand to make reservations except in peak summer (including Christmas and January) travel season and Easter, at ski resorts in prime winter months, or at the top lodges.

If you're driving, the best accommodation values in many parts of New Zealand are farm holidays ($NZ90-$140 double per night with breakfast and dinner) and non-farm homestays

(NZ$60 double B&B or NZ$60-$70 per person including all meals). Pick the type of farm you wish to visit (sheep, dairying, cattle, cropping or high country), and share meals with the hosts. Take part in farm activities if you wish. Reservations, which are essential, can be made through U.S. travel agents or directly. Contact:

Farm Holidays Ltd., P.O. Box 1436, Wellington, tel. 723-2126;

Farmhouse Holidays, Kitchener Rd., Milford, Auckland tel. 492-171;

New Zealand Farm Holidays, Private Bag, Parnell, Auckland, tel. 394-780;

Farm Home and Country Home Holidays, Box 31-250, Auckland, tel. 492-171;

Home Stay/Farm Stay, P.O. Box 630, Rotorua, tel. 24-895, including non-farm homes throughout the North Island;

Town and Country Home Hosting, Box 143, Cambridge, tel. 27-6511;

Rural Tours, P.O. Box 228, Cambridge, tel. 07-127;

Rural Holidays New Zealand, P.O. Box 2155, Christchurch, tel. 61-919;

Friendly Kiwi Home Hosting Service, P.O. Box 5049, Port Nelson, tel. 85-575;

N.Z. Home Hospitality, P.O. Box 309, Nelson, tel. 84-727, also offering non-farm homestays throughout both islands; and

New Zealand Travel Hosts, 279 Williams St., Kaiapoi, tel. 6340, for home hosting.

Get a copy of the *New Zealand Accommodation Guide* from the NZTP office in Auckland for a listing of individual farms and home hosts.

Motel flats/tourist flats (complete apartments) usually include two bedrooms, a living room, a fully equipped kitchen, and a bathroom with shower for NZ$35-$49 double (low-price), with a pool and spa on the premises. Medium priced motels cost NZ$50-$69. Serviced motels—rather Spartan motel rooms—cost slightly less than tourist flats.

An economical way to book hotels is as part of an airline package that also includes a rental car and a quality hotel for a fixed price. The best deal for independent travelers that any of the airlines or travel packagers offers in low season (April to the end of September) is $1370 for round-trip airfare, seven nights accommodations and seven days car rental with unlimited mileage. The price goes up to $1620 in the December through March high season. Each additional day, the average per-day cost goes down as the airfare is amortized over the longer stay. If you want to stay at a premium hotel, you pay a daily supplement of about NZ$30 per person/share twin. The same is true for farm stays. After the initial seven day package, use this guide's day-by-day suggestions.

One of the better package deals for independent travelers in New Zealand is Best Western Motel, Hotel and Motor Inn vouchers combined with a low-cost car rental voucher. Purchase accommodation vouchers directly from Best Western at a cost of US$30 per voucher for one or two persons per room per day. Send a check or money order, 30 days in advance of departure, to **Best Western**, P.O. Box 10203, Accounting Pass Dept., Phoenix, Ariz. 85064. The same vouchers cost more purchased through a wholesaler, with or without a car.

Quality Inns has launched a New Zealand hotel pass plan that enables travelers to get discounts from 20% to 50% off regular rates at its 13 properties. Purchase a minimum of five vouchers in the U.S., each costing US$70 (including tax) for one to three persons, and use them any time during the calendar year at the same hotel or five different properties. Make a reservation for the first night in Auckland before leaving the U.S. and the rest (for example, in Rotorua, Wellington, Christchurch and Queenstown) after arrival in New Zealand.

Bed-and-breakfast guesthouses and small hotels provide lodging and breakfast for under NZ$60 double. The hospitality and helpfulness typically are wonderful, and the other guests are the kind of New Zealanders and visitors you want to meet. Depending on the locality and season, booking may be difficult. One of the advantages of following this itinerary is that you can book ahead and be assured of getting the ones you want.

Motor camps, with communal bathroom, laundry and kitchen facilities, are a terrific value. They offer tent and caravan sites from NZ$4-$7 per person, a few cabins or A-frames from NZ$15-$28 double (provide your own sleeping bag), on-site caravans from about NZ$15 single or double, and sometimes flats from about NZ$28 for two or three persons (no linen). If you're an AAA member, which I advise for drivers, stop by any Automobile Association office for their *Accommodation, Camping and Breakdown Guide to the South Island, Accommodation and Camping Guide South Island, AAA North Island Outdoor Guide, New Zealand Holiday Parks Guide to N.Z. Camp Caravan and Cabin Accommodation*, and the directory of the Camp & Cabin Association.

Youth hostels, everything from farmhouses to modern buildings, are in excellent locations throughout the country. "Youth" can include anyone over five years old with a membership, which you can purchase either before you leave the U.S. or in New Zealand. Additional advantages of membership include discounts on car rentals, rail and ferry rides, ski packages and other outdoor activities, and tour packages with YHA accommodations and transporation. Contact **Australia House**, 36 Customs St. East, Auckland to find out about current membership benefits.

All youth hostel prices quoted in the itinerary are for "Seniors" (over 18). With your sleeping bag and pillowcase, bunk beds are available in dorms sharing communal facilities, priced from NZ$9 to NZ$12 per person. Maximum stay is three nights, facilities are closed during the day, curfew time usually is 10:30 p.m. except in major cities, and help with cleanup is expected. Book in advance during vacation and school holiday periods, especially in popular tourist areas. Send a money order for the first night, along with an international reply coupon, to National Reservations Centre, P.O. Box 436, Christchurch. A **Wanderlust Pass** for discounts can be obtained from YHA offices in Auckland, Wellington and Christchurch together with a handbook to New Zealand's Hostels.

YMCAs and YWCAs are a very attractive budget option in major cities and towns, starting at about NZ$19 per person with breakfast and dinner. Although many students live in them, these facilities frequently are less crowded, even during peak season, and offer more privacy, with some private or shared rooms.

At the other end of the budget spectrum are luxury and first-class hotels, many operated by international hotel chains, and sporting lodges that offer unique facilities and experiences for fishing and hunting enthusiasts. Book hotel reservations at the time you make international air reservations in order to obtain discount packages or discounts offered by the airlines. Superior and luxury class hotels in New Zealand are easy to locate and book through their U.S. sales centers. The best are the Tourist Hotel Corporation of New Zealand's (THC, 35 Albert St., Auckland, tel. 773-689) uniquely located, one-of-a-kind facilities.

Many modern, high standard hotels and motor inns in all major and secondary tourist areas cost NZ$70-$100 single. The NZTP or DAA offices will gladly book them for you after your arrival in Auckland. The same is true for all of my recommended accommodations, which start at NZ$70 and go downward.

Where and What to Eat
The New Zealand eating experience that should not be missed is a Maori *hangi* (feast) in Rotorua, which features many steamed dishes and Maori entertainment.

Surprisingly few restaurants do justice to the quality of New Zealand meat or seafood. In or out of restaurants, the foods to look for are: roast spring lamb (especially October-January), steaks and roast beef, farm-raised venison, tasty and inexpensive meat and savory pies (egg and bacon, mincemeat), and great seafood—five varieties of blue cod, fresh plump bluff oysters in the winter and small sweet Auckland rock oysters, Marlborough scallops in spring and summer, crayfish, marinated mussels year-round, smoked and fresh salmon, John Dory, orange roughy, grouper, kingfish, flounder, snapper and squid. Look for melons in summer, kiwi fruit in winter and spring, fresh vegetables and all kinds of berries.

Though New Zealand is not on the international gourmet tour circuit, French-New Zealand or French provincial cuisine in and near the major cities is quite respectable and, in some instances, outstanding.

Stay at a bed-and-breakfast and the quantity of good food may even carry you until dinner. Otherwise wait until tea-time (after 10:00 a.m.) to snack with your tea or coffee. For lunch I recommend eating places in each city and town for light lunches (about NZ$5-$7), but look carefully at each day's schedule to see if an economical takeout picnic lunch at a park or beach from a local deli wouldn't be more fun. Tourist spots are full of pubs and take-aways, and every town of any size has its Cobb & Co. with reasonable prices. Many of the best dinner spots are unpretentious BYOs (bring your own wine). Most "splurge" restaurants are licensed to serve liquor, except on Sundays, and dress-up is expected. You don't have to tip anywhere, but if the service is good, a tip is appreciated.

Information Sources
Information to supplement this book is available from the New Zealand Tourist and Publicity (NZTP) Office nearest you:
Suite 1530, 10960 Wilshire Blvd., Los Angeles, CA 90024.
Suite 970, Alcoa Building, 1 Maritime Plaza, San Francisco, CA 94111.
Suite 530, 630 Fifth Avenue, New York, NY 10111.
If you're planning a visit longer than 30 days, contact the consulate in the same buildings as the NZTP.

New Zealand Travel Offices, providing information and complete travel services, are located in:
Auckland (tel. 09-798-180)
Rotorua (tel. 073-85-179)
Wellington (tel. 04-739-269)
Christchurch (tel. 03-794-900)
Dunedin (tel. 024-740-344)
Queenstown (tel. 143/379)

Every city and larger town has a public relations office (PRO) and visitors information centre. AAA members can collect maps and information for every square kilometer of New Zealand, and also book everything, at the New Zealand Automobile Association:

    Auckland (tel. 09-774-660)
    Wellington (tel. 04-851-745)
    Christchurch (tel. 03-791-280)
    Dunedin (tel. 024-775-945)

To call any of these numbers from the U.S., dial the country code (64), then the area codes. When dialing within New Zealand, include the zero before the city's code.

Suggested Reading

Supplement *22 Days in New Zealand* with other travel guide-books for background and detail. Two completely different New Zealand travel guides stand out: the photographs, historical and cultural treatment, as well as interesting and balanced travel narrative, of Insight Guides' *New Zealand*, APA, 1986; and Jane King's *New Zealand Handbook*, Moon Publications, 1987, in a class by itself for thoroughness. Both books include extensive and balanced reading lists. Travelers watching their budgets especially owe Ms. King a debt of gratitude. Her book's detail and travel options even surpass those in Tony Wheeler's excellent *New Zealand: A Travel Survival Kit*, Lonely Planet, 1985.

    Susan Poole's *Frommer's New Zealand on $25 A Day*, Simon & Schuster, 1987, is also a bargain. *Fodor's New Zealand 1987* covers only tourist highlights in a super-condensed text. Sunset's *New Zealand Travel Guide*, Lane Publications, 1987, is well-organized and readable, with a good collection of maps and photos.

    Claire Jones' *New Zealand's Bay of Islands: The Land and Sea Guide*, published by Roger and Evelyn Miles (owners of Rainbow Charters, Opua), provides detailed touring information, business telephone numbers, nautical charts and superb photos of the Bay of Islands. It is only available in New Zealand.

NEW ZEALAND IS UNIQUE

Flora and Fauna

When New Zealand broke away from Australia and Antarctica, about 70 million years ago, its geographic isolation ensured a unique assortment of animals and plant life not found elsewhere. Dense forests with 112 native tree species and thick undergrowth supported 250 species of native birds, many flightless, that grazing animals and predators introduced by settlers reduced dramatically. Many of the species released by European settlers, like cats, weasels, deer, opossums, pigs and hares, live in Urewera National Park, the North Island's largest forest.

The most famous survivor is the flightless, nocturnal kiwi, New Zealand's national emblem, named after its piercing whistle, "keee-weee." You're more likely to hear than see the kiwi in the bush, especially in the middle of the night, so look for it in nocturnal houses such as at Auckland's zoo. The kiwi is only one of several remaining flightless birds, including the kakapo, kea, waka and the very rare blue and iridescent green takahe, thought to be extinct until a colony was rediscovered in Fiordland, where all of these birds live, along with the rare southern crested grebe and the Fiordland crested penguin.

At lower elevations, you'll find New Zealand's version of pampas grass, toe toe, along with rimu, northern rate and tawa forest, fading to beech, totara and tawari above 2600 feet. This vegetation shelters three species of parrot—kaka, morepork and red-crowned and yellow-crowned parakeet—and the white-breasted kereru, New Zealand's only native pigeon, easily sighted here or in Tongariro National Park because it makes a loud flapping noise when it flies.

The kaka is a very shy brown and green parrot, quite unlike the personality of the daring kea, a flightless parrot which lives mainly in the Southern Alps. The scavenging kea will tear anything in your campsite or on your car that it can get its hooked beak into. Equally bold but not as common, the flightless Weka may be seen trashing campsites in the west coast of the South Island and on the east coast of the North Island, around Gisborne.

In each of the mountain areas you'll visit on the North and South Islands, variations in climate (wet side and dry side) and altitude produce distinctive vegetation zones. In Tongariro National Park (Day 9), Urewera National Park and Egmont National Park on the North Island, and the Southern Alps from Arthur's Pass National Park to Fiordland National Park, a green canopy of broadleaf rainforests, with thick undergrowth, yields through several different forest zones to shrub, tussock and alpine herb zones, sprinkles with buttercups and daisies, before only lichen can survive below permanent snowlines.

From north to south there are many different birds, but always abundant. Native songbirds, like the tui and bellbird, can be heard below the 3000-foot level in Tongariro's rainforests, their rapturous songs managing to crest above the noisy cicadas, except in their deafening summer crescendo. Watch for the blue duck, an endangered species, near streams flowing swiftly through the broadleafs, small and huge fern trees (up to 30 feet high), vines and other exotic greenery. In Westland National Park (Day 20), tui and bellbird songs are joined by fantail, tomtit, oyster-catchers, terns, godwits and white herons breeding in the coastal wetlands from October to February.

In Fiordland National Park and Mt. Aspiring National Park, birdwatchers can look for banded dotterels, black-billed gulls, black-fronted terns, yellow hammers, mallards, paradise ducks, shining cuckoos, yellow heads, song thrushes and dozens of others also common to other areas.

There are more than 150 species of ferns in New Zealand, growing everywhere together with mostly white or cream-colored flowers, including 60 species of orchids. Stewart Island alone has 30 species and a wealth of other native plants and rare birds like kakas, Stewart Island robins, Stewart Island brown kiwis, fernbirds, plied shags, Stewart Island shags, yellow-eyed penguins and the kakapo, also found in Fiordland.

About 500 species of alpine flowers are found only in New Zealand. Above the 3000-foot level, the tiny green rifleman and silver eye inhabit the beeches, safely below the sub-alpine tussock shrublands minutely searched for small birds and animals by native falcons. In December and January, birds of Tongariro's tussockland fly over vast acreages of alpine flora blooming white with touches of purple or mauve orchids. In December you'll see the pohutukawa (New Zealand Christmas Tree) bloom, and in spring the parasitic rata's red blossoms and the bright yellow Kowhai blossoms. Aging gnarled pohutu-kawas form the backdrop of Auckland's sandy bays tucked between headlands on the eastern shoreline.

New Zealand's native kauri is a conifer, botanically in the pine and fir family of less magnificent trees found in Australia, Malaysia and Pacific Islands. The kauri's lower branches and bark shed leaving a massive crown of leathery leaves as high as 150 feet above the large mound of humus covering its root system. Settlers and shipbuilders depleted most kauri forests of these giants that require about 800 years to mature. However, surviving and now protected kauri groves still can be seen west of Auckland in the Waitakera Ranges (Day 3), around Russell (Day 5) and west of Kerikeri (Day 6), north of Dargaville (Day 6) and on the Cormandel Peninsula (Day 7).

No discussion of New Zealand flora and fauna would be complete without mentioning the islands' most common mammals —sheep. More than 70 million sheep dot the countryside, about 20 sheep for every New Zealander. New Zealand is the third largest producer and the second largest exporter of wool in the world. Sheep are raised for wool in the hill country, with lamb and mutton production in the low country. In 1850-80, while Maori tribes and the government on the North Island were at war over land, huge tracts of the South Island's tussockland were rapidly being occupied by Australian Merino sheep farmers. Sheep scab disease, a plague of rabbits and the discovery of gold in the 1860s slowed expansion of sheep grazing. But the introduction of refrigeration and refrigerated cargo ships in the early 1880s spurred lamb-breeding for overseas meat consumers.

At the Agrodome in Rotorua, the sheep station in Queenstown, and other locations, sheep herders put talented sheep dogs through their paces with vocal and whistle commands. Professional sheep-shearers show how it's done.

New Zealand's Volcanic Legacy

Volcanoes dominate the Auckland-Cormandel Peninsula landscape from air, sea and land. Symmetrical Rangitoto Island, guarding the entrance to Auckland's Waitemata Harbour, erupted a mere 200 years ago. Auckland itself is situated on a plateau marked by 60 volcanic cones around which early Maori settlements clustered for defense. The volcanic ramparts of the Waitakeres rise to the west, descending to black sandy beaches on the western shores pounded by Tasman breakers. Today these are parks and reserves, among the best viewpoints. The Cormandel Ranges are volcanic stumps rising steeply east of the Firth of Thames. Volcanic remnants still exist, and on Day 6 you'll dig hot water pools around Hot Water Beach.

Polynesian voyagers from "Hawaiki" landed their canoe, *Te Awara*, at Maketu (south of what is today Tauranga—Day 7) on the Bay of Plenty in the middle of the 14th century. According to legend, Ngatoroirangi traveled south to Tongariro and, when close to freezing to death in a snowstorm, called on his sisters in Hawaiki to bring warmth. His route south is marked by geothermal activity, from the active volcano Whakaari (White Island) through the geysers, steaming cliffs, bubbling pools of mud and hot springs spurting from the ground around Rotorua and Lake Taupo, to the active volcanoes of Tongariro National Park. The Maori had been using the healing properties of local mineral hot pools, the "healing springs," 500 years before tourists were first drawn to Rotorua's thermal wonders, especially the Pink and White Terraces of Lake Rotomahana, produced by hydro-thermal changes in the pumice, and destroyed by the eruption of Tarawera in 1886.

Maori Art, Crafts and Settlements

The earliest history of New Zealand is linked to ancestors of the Maoris from eastern Polynesia. Maori mythology has Kupe discovering Aotearoa in about 950 AD followed about four hundred years later by the armada of canoes to which Maori tribes trace their geneologies. Archeological remains suggest that as early as 1000 AD Maori hunters of huge, now-extinct flightless birds (moa) roamed the coastal South Island. The giant moa offered plentiful food and forests yielded huge trees (kauri) for carving dugout canoes and construction of dwellings. Later as the moas became rare, tribal and sub-tribal groups settled in villages.

Pas are fortified settlements built by a large family or part of a tribe, housing the local chief and his warband and also serving as a dwelling place, a food storage facility, a center for craftsmen and a refuge against attack. Located on a defensible high point, coastal headland or the edge of a swamp, the *pa* and its surroundings were fortified with earthworks, scarping on the sides and ditches, with living quarters on artificial terraces. *Pas* were built and used from the late 15th or early 16th centuries to the early 1800s. *Pas* can be seen in the Bay of Islands, Kerikeri, Russell, the Auckland isthmus, the Bay of Plenty, Waikato, Taranaki (southwest) and Hawke's Bay (southeast) on the North Island.

The years that followed European settlement opened a period of constructing communal meeting houses (*whare whakairo*) for social purposes and to discuss many problems: fighting with settlers, British, and other tribes; land problems; disease; guns, and so forth. These meeting houses are highly ornamented displays of Maori wood-carving skills. See for example: the Tama-te Kapua at Ohinemutu, in Rotorua; Poho-o Rawiri, the largest meeting house in New Zealand, near Gisbourne; Te Hauki Turanga in the National Museum (originally built in Poverty Bay); Hotunui in the Auckland Museum; and the Waitangi Treaty House on the Waitangi Peninsula.

The greenstone rocks that you can see in Auckland and Hokitika's factories on the South Island's west coast are only found in New Zealand in the Arahura and Taramakau riverbeds flowing from the Southern Alps to the Tasman Sea. Greenstone was so revered by Maori tribes for tools, ornaments and weapons that they trekked over the Alps to the west coast to collect it and fought wars for it. The stone is so iron-hard that Maori would have to spend months or even years working it with water and sandstone, or much longer to perfect a *mere*—a flat, pointed weapon imbued with *mana* (power) in the process of crafting it for tribal chiefs.

When Captain Cook arrived in Northland in 1769, Maori culture and arts were at their peak. No tour of New Zealand would be complete without seeing some examples of traditional Maori art and crafts from this classic period housed primarily in North Island museums. In addition to wood carving, the Maoris worked in stone, clay, feathers and fiber.

In the last hundred years, much of the native genius infusing the most marvelous artistic aspect of Maori culture have suffered inevitable attrition in the process of conflict with and assimilation by *pakehas* (Europeans). However, the Maori's unique visual arts legacy still lives on, fostered by intensifying Maori and national efforts to sustain and revive the traditions.

Maori culture and artistic accomplishments are most visible on the North Island and in Rotorua, supplemented by visits to national and regional museums and meeting house sites, including: Auckland's War Memorial Museum; regional museums at Dargaville, Matakohe, Russell and Kaitaia in the Northland; the Taranaki Museum in New Plymouth; Hawke's Bay Museum and Art Gallery; North Island Regional Museum in Wanganui; Wellington's National Museum and Art Gallery; Christchurch's Canterbury Museum; and Dunedin's Otago Museum.

ITINERARY

DAY 1 Arrive in Auckland in the morning, get set up in your accommodation, then relax and enjoy a leisurely visit to Queen Street, the spine of downtown, sidestreets climbing the hillsides. Have a snack lunch at the waterfront, then visit the Auckland Visitor's Bureau, the NZ Government Tourist Bureau or AA New Zealand for information, brochures, maps, and reservations as needed for North and South Island accommodations. After dinner, call it quits early to beat jet lag.

DAY 2 Downtown Auckland's attractions can be seen in a full morning. Start with city views from either One Tree Hill or Mt. Eden. If you feel energetic and the weather is pleasant, walk along portions of the Coast-to-Coast Walkway from Waitomata Harbor to Manakau Harbor. Highlights include Albert Park, Auckland Domain and the War Memorial Museum and Wintergardens. Visit the Parnell District for lunch, followed by a walking tour among its Edwardian and Victorian houses renovated as boutiques. Afterwards head down to the harbor for a cruise in the Hauraki Gulf Maritime Park. After returning to Auckland's harborfront, briefly visit the Old Auckland Customhouse before taking a 20-minute ride on the Devonport Ferry to the North Shore for sunset views from North Head or Mt. Victoria, followed by dinner in Devonport. Return to downtown Auckland on the ferry.

DAY 3 Take the Waitakere Range Scenic Drive, west of Auckland, to Pahi's black-sand beach along the Tasman Sea. For lunch and winetasting, visit Henderson Valley vineyards in the western suburbs. Then drive east to the North Shore's beaches and bays en route to the Waiwera hot mineral pools, 30 miles north of Auckland. After a relaxing dip, head back to your hotel to get ready for a special dinner on Ponsonby Road.

DAY 4 Leave early for the Bay of Islands and make scenic side-trips on the way north. Following Highway 1, exit to the east for Sandspit where the ferry departs for beautiful, historic Kawau Island. Returning to Highway 1, make two more scenic detours: one to Mangawhai Heads and the other through Whangarei to Whangarei Heads. Then continue north along the Tutukaka Coast, which loops back to the main highway. Head for the car ferry to Russell at Opua. If all goes according to plan, you'll arrive in Russell in time to stretch your legs climbing to the summit of Maki Hill for a panoramic view of the town and its surroundings at sunset before indulging in a delicious local seafood dinner. In the evening, enjoy a few hours at the Duke of

Marlborough Pub, relaxing and listening to big game fishing conversation. Stay overnight in Russell.

DAY 5 After a leisurely breakfast in Russell, take an all-morning Cream Trip cruise to the outer limits of the Bay of Islands, including a picnic lunch at Otehei Bay on Urupukaouka Island. In the afternoon, head for Kerikeri via Paihia, historic Waitangi and beautiful Haruru Falls. Sightsee along Kerikeri Inlet's beautiful shoreline, bays and coves before dinner at the Stone Store Restaurant. Overnight in Kerikeri.

DAY 6 Today will be a long day of driving and sightseeing. Check out early and head to the west coast to see the Waipoua Kauri Sanctuary's huge and ancient kauri trees. Further south, on the way back to Auckland, stop at Dargaville's Northern Wairoa Museum and the outstanding Otamatea Kauri and Pioneer Museum in Matakoke. Instead of driving to Rotorua via Hamilton, which is the fastest and most direct route from Auckland, drive 75 miles southeast of Auckland to Thames on the Coromandel Peninsula. Check in and enjoy a late but leisurely dinner overlooking the Firth of Thames.

DAY 7 From Thames, head north along the rugged coast for breakfast in Coromandel overlooking the harbor. Afterwards you have a choice of heading east on unpaved Highway 309 through stunning mountain scenery across the peninsula, or heading north to view the breathtaking coastal scenery from Colville to Fletcher Bay. Further north, around the peninsula past lovely Port Charles Harbor, enjoy the beautiful white sands of Whangapou, the pink sands of New Chums Beach, Hahei and Hot Water Beach. Stop to dig your own thermal hot pools and have a picnic lunch. After lunch move on to Whitianga, renowned for big game fishing, diving and underwater photography, and then to even more spectacular coastline from Mercury Bay to Waihi Beach. From Waihi Beach, follow the Bay of Plenty through Tauranga and Mount Maunganui. Then turn inland from the Bay of Plenty's beaches to Rotorua.

DAY 8 In Rotorua you're in the midst of an amazing thermal region. Explore an incredible assortment of geysers, hot springs, steaming cliffs and boiling mud pools. Visit trout pools in beautiful forest parks fed by enormous quantities of spring water. Learn about Maori culture, arts and crafts in New Zealand's largest concentration of Maoris and their national cultural center. After experiencing these thermal wonders (possibly including a flightseeing trip that lands on Mount Tarawera's summit), enjoy the unique experience of a Maori *hangi* feast and entertainment in Rotorua.

DAY 9 Leave early in the morning for a drive to Aratiatia Rapids and Huka Falls on the Waikato River and a visit to the geothermal power project to the south, all on the way to Taupo. After lunch in Taupo, drive to Turangi to spend a while trout fishing in the Tongariro River and its tributaries, or to watch trout from behind glass in a trout hatchery. Then drive along Tongariro National Park to Ohakune, the center of park activities, and up the slopes of Mt. Ruapehu. Afterwards continue driving to Wanganui to visit one of the most picturesque cities in New Zealand, aptly called the "Garden City."

DAY 10 The parks and gardens of Wanganui are a perfect place to gear down and relax. Visit to the Wanganui Museum, one of the country's best regional museums. Then have a picnic lunch in beautiful Virginia Lake Park. After lunch take a paddlewheeler trip to Holly Lodge East Winery and from there a jetboat ride to Hipango Park. After returning to Wanganui, drive south past a string of scenic beach settlements along the Tasman Sea to New Zealand's capital city of Wellington.

DAY 11 Set in a green amphitheater on a sparkling harbor, Wellington is at its best viewed from the heights of Mount Victoria and from 24-mile Marine Drive and Miramar Peninsula, stopping along the way for a picnic lunch. Spend the afternoon touring downtown Wellington, including Parliament Buildings and the National Museum. In the late afternoon, take the cable car up to Kelburn terminal for a stroll through the Botanic Gardens followed by dinner overlooking the city and harbor.

DAY 12 Sail early on the Inter-Island Ferry (with breakfast on board) across Cook Strait from Wellington to Picton at the head of Queen Charlotte Sound in Marlborough Sounds. Trains and buses await those without cars. The trip to Christchurch takes five to six hours. Dinner in this English city setting is followed by a stroll along the beautiful Avon River to parks, gardens and other urban attractions within a few blocks of the tree-shaded riverbanks.

DAY 13 Tour the inner city and outskirts of Christchurch. Visit the Botanic Gardens, Hadley Park and Cathedral Square. Perhaps rent a canoe and follow the Avon for a tour of local architecture, stopping for a riverside picnic lunch. In the afternoon, make a round trip on the scenic North and South Summit Road to Lyttelton Harbor. Pass through Port Hills for wonderful sunset views while strolling on bush walkways. Return to your hotel to get ready for dinner and an evening of entertainment at the Christchurch Arts Centre.

DAY 14 This morning travel south across sheep-covered plains from Christchurch through Fairlie and Burke's Pass, past the blue-green and turquoise glacial Lakes Tekapo and Pukaki to Mount Cook National Park. Trampers, climbers, rafters and skiers will find a feast of activities. After lunch, if at all possible, take a ski-plane flightseeing trip to the Tasman Glacier. Upon returning, drive through the tussock-covered expanses of the Mackenzie Basin, with a brief stop at Lake Oahu. Follow the Southern Alps over Lindis Pass to Queenstown, gateway to the wonders of Fiordland.

DAY 15 Few places in the world have more variety of year-round lake, mountain and river recreational attractions than Queenstown and vicinity. After breakfast and booking excursions in the town center, start the day with a leisurely cruise on beautiful Lake Wakatipu on the coal-burning *T.S.S. Earnslaw*. A trip to Queenstown would not be complete without a jetboat or white-water rafting trip on one of Otago's gold-bearing rivers. After lunch in Arrowtown, a pretty relic of the gold mining era, take a horsetrek to Moke Lake or spend an exciting afternoon traveling by four-wheel vehicle up Skippers Canyon above the Shotover River. In the evening, a gondola ride from the town center up to Bob's Peak for dinner and spectacular views of the lake, mountains and Queenstown completes a perfect day.

DAY 16 With an early start from Queenstown, head for Te Anau and Lake Manapouri. The first stop in Te Anau is the Fiordland National Park Headquarters. After a picnic lunch in one of Lake Te Anau's most picturesque inlets, visit Te Anau Caves' glow-worm caves, or take a launch tour of the West Arm followed by a bus or floatplane trip to Doubtful Sound for a two-hour launch cruise. In the evening have a relaxing dinner in Te Anau.

DAY 17 Rudyard Kipling aptly described Milford Sound as "the eighth wonder of the world." It is three memorable hours from Te Anau to Milford through Eglinton and Hollyford Valleys and the Homer Tunnel, culminating in a magnificent one to two hour Milford Sound launch cruise with views of Mitre Peak and Sutherland Falls. Drive your own car and, on the way back, you can spend extra time at several lakes and take a short hike on one of the tracks (Hollyford, Greenstone or Routebourne). Finish the day with dinner in Te Anau or have a camper's meal along one of the tracks.

DAY 18 Backtrack to Queenstown and, in good weather, drive up the unpaved road to the top of the Crown Range, then through Cardrona Valley in time for lunch in Wanaka. Climb up Mt. Iron for the view. There's still time for superb trout or salmon fishing in Lakes Wanaka or Hawea, kayaking on the Motatapu River, horse-trekking or, in winter, afternoon skiing on Cardrona. The Wanaka waterfront and nearby Glendhu Bay are great places for after-dinner sunset strolls.

DAY 19 Leave Wanaka very early for a full-day's drive down Makarora Valley, over Haast Pass and then to the National Park Centre at Fox Glacier in South Westland. Plan on making the not-too-strenuous climb to Fox Chalet Lookout for inspiring views of Fox Glacier and the Tasman Sea at sunset. Move on to Franz Josef Glacier for dinner and overnight.

DAY 20 Have a hearty breakfast and leave by minibus for the 2 ½ hour Franz Josef Glacier Valley Walk. Later, on the way up the narrow Westland coastal strip to Hokitika, visit Lake Matheson, Lake Kaniere Reserve or some of the other beautiful small lakes en route. Spend the afternoon in the Hokitika area visiting relics of the gold mining era, factories cutting greenstone (the Maori sacred gemstone), and several superb viewpoints, before driving to Greymouth for the night.

DAY 21 Visit Shantytown's reconstruction of an 1860s gold mining town near Greymouth. Then drive on to Highway 73, Arthur's Pass Road, the most spectacular of the South Island's alpine crossings, passing through Arthur's Pass National Park. Plan for a lunch stop near Arthur's Pass Village, scenic walks on several inspiring trails, and perhaps a last trout fishing excursion at Pearson Lake. Descend to Christchurch to check in and prepare for dinner in Christchurch.

DAY 22 In the morning head for Banks Peninsula, with beautiful coastal stretches dotted with sleepy towns. Enjoy lunch and sightseeing in Akaroa, the charming Victorian village with an historic touch of French in its architecture and signs. On the way back to Christchurch in the afternoon, stop at Okains Bay and several other villages on the Peninsula. Celebrate the conclusion of the trip this evening with a deluxe dinner in Christchurch.

DAY 1
ARRIVE IN AUCKLAND

Welcome to New Zealand! Ease into the comfortable Kiwi
lifestyle and pace. Spend the day in Auckland settling into your
hotel and getting acquainted with the central city, Parnell and
the harborfront. While you're on Queen Street, stop at the New
Zealand Tourist and Publicity travel office (NZTP) to book
future accommodations, transportation, sightseeing and other
tours in the Auckland region and elsewhere in New Zealand,
and gather information and maps for the rest of your trip.

Suggested Schedule

Arrive at Auckland International Airport.
Take a bus or taxi downtown or directly to
your accommodations and check in.
Enjoy a relaxing breakfast or lunch in Parnell
before exploring the city.
Book future accommodations, transportation
and excursions at the NZTP office.
Ease into Auckland's night life with the expec-
tation of an early start the next morning.

Auckland Orientation
Auckland straddles a narrow isthmus between two harbors:
Manukau on the west and Waitemata on the east merging into
Hauraki Gulf. The Harbour Bridge across Waitemata Harbour
links the city with the rapidly growing North Shore. Over a
quarter of New Zealand's population (850,000) lives in Auckland, mostly in single-story houses, an urbanized network of
villages sprawling over a hilly region of volcanoes. A large
Maori community and immigrants from Europe, Asia and the
Pacific Islands give Auckland a cosmopolitan flavor. With over
70,000 Polynesians, Auckland is the world's largest Polynesian
center. Niueans and Cook Islanders, Samoans and Tongans add
interest and vitality to city life.
      See the city tomorrow from several vantage points: the twin
cones of Mt. Victoria and North Head across the Waitemata Harbour; One Tree Hill and Mt. Eden, part of a Coast-to-Coast
Walkway from Waitemata Harbour to Manakau Harbour; and
the Waitakere Scenic Drive west of the city Discover Auckland's
beautiful parks, especially Victorian Albert Park in the city
center and Cornwall Park, with sheep and cattle grazing on its

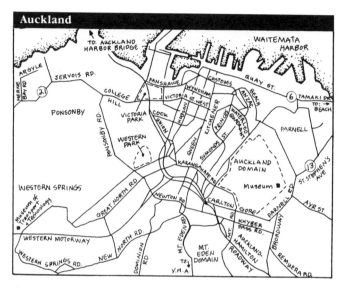

Auckland

slopes, which merges with One Tree Hill.

Lower Queen Street is downtown Auckland's main street. From the Ferry Terminal on wide and busy Quay Street, Queen Street is filled with shops, arcades and offices. The street has little charm but plenty of choices. From the Ferry Terminal, catch the ferry to Devonport on the North Shore or, from nearby wharves, launch trips to Haura Ki Gulf Islands. Queen Elizabeth Square at the bottom of Queen Street contains the central post office, downtown complex (more stores and the city's duty-free shop) and offices.

Browse in craft shops, antique stores, art galleries and boutiques in the suburbs of Parnell along Parnell Road, with its renovated Victorian and Edwardian buildings, as well as in Remuera, Ponsonby, Victoria Park Market's food and craft market, and colorful Karangahape Road, opposite Grafton Bridge, where many Pacific Islanders shop.

If you arrive on Saturday, Auckland's downtown is best seen before noon, when many shops, cafes and restaurants close. If you arrive on Sunday, take the day off like everyone else. Depending on the weather, join the droves heading for beaches and the ocean. Otherwise, get lost in the fabulous War Memorial Museum.

From Airport to Accommodations

Auckland International Airport lies 13 miles south of the city. The terminal contains a Travellers' Information Centre (tel.

275-7467) open Monday to Sunday, 6:30 a.m. to 11:00 p.m., bank, post office, rental car desk and even a rental shower.

Between 6:00 a.m. and 9:00 p.m., coaches leave regularly for the Downtown Airline Terminal at the corner of Quay and Albert Streets. The fare is NZ$4. On request, the driver will drop you off at city hotels on the direct bus route. Taxi fares to downtown are about NZ$25 on weekdays and slightly higher on weekends. Touristop Tourist Services Ltd. in the Downtown Airline Terminal is open all week from 8:30 a.m. to 4:30 p.m. (tel. 775-783). Deplaning in Auckland on the weekend without a room reservation can be a problem. The Travellers' Information Centre at the Airport will book accommodations or, after arriving in downtown Auckland, turn immediately to the New Zealand Government Tourist Bureau (NZGTB), 99 Queen Street (tel. 798-180), for booking assistance (8:30 a.m. to 5:00 p.m. weekdays and 9:30 a.m. to noon on Saturdays). NZGTB has a NZ$2 booking fee. The Automobile Association, 33 Wyndham St. (tel. 774-660), can be just as helpful if you bring your U.S. AAA membership card. The Auckland Youth Hostel (YH) office, open from 8:30 a.m. to 4:30 p.m., is in Australia House, 36 Customs Street East (794-224), very close to the Bus Terminal and the Percy Shieff Hostel (790-258). The Best Western/New Zealand Reservation Service (tel. 792-854) provides 24-hour booking service and has numerous properties in the Auckland area with NZ$40-$50 rates.

In addition to the NZGTB, the Auckland Visitors' Bureau, 299 Queen Street at Aotea Square, has all the maps, information and guidebooks you could possibly need for the next few days, including brochures on Auckland's latticework of signposted walkways, parks, reserves, botanic gardens and dozens of gulf islands.

City Transporation

A car is convenient but not essential to see Auckland. You don't have to rent a car until Day 3. Buses of the Auckland Regional Authority (ARA) and suburban companies run frequently to most in-town and outlying locations from the Downtown Bus Centre (tel. 797-119 between 6:00 a.m. and 11:00 p.m. for information) on Commerce Street behind the main post office and other downtown locations. In addition to the main ARA terminal, there are four suburban centers: in New Lynn, Onehunga, Panmure, and Otahuhu. Timetables and tickets can be obtained from kiosks at these locations or The Bus Place (131 Hobson Street, Mon.-Fri., 8:15 a.m. to 4:30 p.m.). Call Buz-a-Bus (tel. 797-119 between 6:00 a.m. and 11:00 p.m. weekdays), tell them where you want to go and they'll provide timetable information.

Ask about 10-trip tickets and family passes for about NZ$5. Busabout Day Pass, which can be bought from a bus driver, costs NZ$4.30 adult, NZ$2 child (or, for two days, NZ$7 adult, NZ$3.60 child) for unlimited ARA bus travel after 9:00 a.m. on weekdays and anytime on weekends and holidays.

For cycle touring, stop by the Visitors Bureau and pick up a bike route map covering about 30 miles around Auckland. Most bike shops around town rent bicycles. On weekends bike rentals are available at The Domain, along the waterfront and in Devonport on the North Shore.

Where to Shop

Parnell's upmarket shopping in one of Auckland's oldest districts benefits from imaginative restoration creating boutiques for fashions, pottery, glassware, jewelry, antiques, various craft items, along with a variety of good quality restaurants and pleasant shops for snacks and refreshments. On and near Parnell Road are historic church buildings, like St. Stephen's and St. Mary's, and some fine old 19th century buildings open to the public. From November to March, see the lovely rose gardens in nearby Sir Dove-Meyer Robinson Park.

Ponsonby's exclusive boutiques stand side-by-side with shops catering to the day-to-day needs of local Polynesians. On Karangahape Road (called "K Road" by local residents) many shops are stocked with Polynesian foods. On Sunday at noon there's a popular market at the corner of K Road and Ponsonby Road. While in the Ponsonby District for shopping or dining, visit Renall Street with about 20 preserved 19th century cottages, privately owned and not open to the public but worth seeing from the outside.

Visit the Otara Shopping Centre car park on Saturday morning for more Polynesian shopping activity.

Cook Street and Victoria Park are busy and entertaining bazaar-style markets. The Cook Street Market is in Aotea Square on Friday from 9:00 a.m. to 8:00 p.m., Saturday from 10:00 a.m. to 4:00 p.m. and Sunday from 10:00 a.m. to 3:00 p.m. Victoria Park Market, Victoria Street West, from 9:00 a.m. to 7:00 p.m. seven days a week, gathers weavers potters, leather workers and other crafts people in the midst of a fruit and vegetable market.

Where to Stay

Start experiencing New Zealand hospitality at a B&B in Auckland. I like staying near Parnell, with its nearby restaurants and cafes and a number of good and inexpensive lodgings. The best B&B bargain is charming **Ascot Parnell**, 36 St. Stephens Ave., Parnell, Auckland, tel. 399-012, a completely restored and well-maintained house dating back to 1910, with spacious, elegant rooms, some with private baths, and complete breakfasts, for NZ$20 single or NZ$39 double. It's well worth booking far in advance.

Another excellent way to start your stay in Auckland is to head from the airport to the cheerful rooms and stained-glass windows of **Heathmaur Lodge**, tel. 763-527, at 75 Argyle St. overlooking Herne Bay. Make reservations in advance for the first night. Otherwise, like many of Auckland's B&Bs, it may be full.

The **Grande Vue**, 3 Princes St., tel. 793-965, opposite the Inter-Continental Hotel, is one of the best in-town budget B&Bs, at about NZ$26 for a single. If all of its 19 units are booked, try the nearby **Arundel Tourist Hotel**, 12 Waterloo Quadrant, tel. 734-828, no longer the best value for budgeteers but full of character and charm, priced at NZ$30 for a B&B single. Single travelers may have a better chance at the **Rosanna Travel Hotel**, 217 Ponsonby Rd., tel. 766-603, with its five single units, NZ$20 with breakfast and without a private bath. Budget travelers with large appetites will love the **Aspen Lodge Bed and Breakfast Tourist Hotel** at 62 Emily Pl., tel. 796-698, from NZ$29 with all-you-can-eat continental breakfasts. **Mt. Eden Youth Hostel**, 5A Oaklands Rd., Mount Eden, tel. 603-975, housing 46 people for NZ$9.50 each per night, is about three miles south of the city center. Take bus number 273, 274 or 275 from the downtown bus station. The **Percy Shieff Youth Hostel**, 7 Princes Street, Auckland, tel. 700-258, for NZ$9.50 per night, has 74 beds in 11 rooms. Located across the street from the Hyatt, it is within walking distance of everything. The **YMCA**, corner of Pitt Street and Grays Avenue, Auckland, tel. 32-068, has singles for men and women, dinner and breakfast, an excellent value at NZ$20.50 per night. Much further from the city, at 14 Shirley Rd., Western Springs, tel. 862-800, but right near Museum of Transport and Technology and the Zoo, with good bus access, **Ivanhoe Travellers Lodge** offers a dorm bed at NZ$9.50 and perfectly adequate single rooms for NZ$14. **Hekerua House**, tel. 72-8371, at Onetangi on Waiheke Island, with private rooms and a dormitory, is the best get-away-from-it-all budget hostel in the region. Rates start at NZ$8.

The **James Cook Motel**, 320 Parnell Road, tel. 33-460, costs NZ$35 for two people. Budget-watchers traveling together who want to be near Parnell Village can find five charming units in a lodge on the **Barrycourt Motor Inn** grounds, 10-20 Gladstone Rd., tel. 33-789, priced at NZ$45 for one or two people. The **Casa Mia**, 481 Parnell Road, tel. 790-436, is small, pleasant and only NZ$16 per night. During university vacations, Spartan budget travelers can try the **Norman Spencer**, 9 St. Stephens

Avenue, Parnell, tel. 799-911, for about NZ$7 single with your own sleeping bag. The **Manor House Hotel**, 363 Queen St., tel. 778-542, has a very convenient location and simple, clean, adequately spacious rooms at NZ$25 single, with a shared bath. With hearty breakfasts that make up for smaller rooms, the **Aspen Lodge**, 62 Emily Place, tel. 796-698, compares favorably with the Manor in all other respects, with NZ$26 singles. **Farthings Hotel**, 131 Beach Rd., tel. 30-629, has a great variety of inexpensive rooms for couples, groups and families of all ages; 75 rooms to choose from starting at NZ$30 for a single without private bath.

Families might prefer **Campbell Court Motel**, across from Cornwall Park, 317 Manukau Rd., Epsom 3, Auckland, tel. 686-409, for units with kitchens, sleeping up to six, laundry facilities, telephones and even color TV. Continental and cooked breakfasts are available. Rates start at NZ$35; each additional person NZ$8; and under 12 NZ$4. Both city and airport buses stop right at the gate. With more units, as well as sauna, swimming and spa pools, the quiet **Mt. Eden Motel**, 47 Balmoral Rd., Mt. Eden, Auckland, tel. 687-187, has about the same rates and also very good bus service.

Where to Eat

Auckland has an underrated collection of restaurants. Even the City's residents are so defensive about their cuisine that the restaurant situation seems much more bleak than it really is. Dining in Auckland may not be one of the best reasons for visiting New Zealand but, especially thanks to the French influence, there are plenty of very good moderate to higher-priced eating places to choose from.

Victoria Park Market, on Victoria St. across from Victoria Park, has pies, hot dogs, pastas, salads and a variety of other standard and ethnic foods for hungry budget travelers. At **Rick's Cafe American** (tel. 399-074) in the market you can count on the potato skins and spare ribs served in Bogart decor. For comparable variety and inexpensive food, the **Plaza Arcade** at 128 Queen St. has 12 international food shops spanning Bali to Britain. **Armadillo's**, 178 Symonds St., tel. 393-744, has huge burgers, good salads and amusing reminders of the old west. If you're a sucker for great pie, try their pecan pie a la mode. For Mexican food, the **Mexican Cafe**, 67 Victoria St. West, tel. 732-311, is the only place to go. After the long climb up Mt. Eden—or even if you drive—try a bowl of **Chez Daniel**'s onion soup at 597 Mt. Eden Road, tel. 689-676.

For inexpensive Italian food, pizza or exotic dishes like chicken stuffed with peanuts, head for **Collage**, right in the heart of town at 26 Lorne Street, tel. 33-086. For even bigger appetites for Italian food, NZ$10 or under, it's **La Bussola**, 17 Great North Road, Ponsonby, tel. 768-597, or **La Tratorria**, 259 Parnell Road, tel. 795-58.

The ten-course buffet lunch, 12:00 noon to 2:30 p.m. weekdays at the **New Orient Restaurant** (Strand Arcade, tel. 797-793), is delicious and less expensive than meals in other Chinese restaurants. Avoid disappointment with seafood fare by heading for the **Union Fish Company**'s old brick warehouse, 16 Quay St., tel. 796-745, replete with maritime decor. You can fit the meal to your pocketbook there, but an even better seafood value is the tiny **Waterfront Cafe**, Ferry Building, Quay St., tel. 732-770. Another top spot for a seafood lunch is **Sitting Duck** in Westhaven Marina (tel. 760-374) which offers top value for the combination of view, menu and price.

Fresh mussels are well-prepared and reasonably priced at the **Front Page Cafe**, 163 Symonds St., tel. 733-579. For innovative seafood menus, visit **Flamingos**, 242 Jervois Road, Herne Bay, tel. 765-899.

Ponsonby Road is the hands-down winner as the street with the greatest number and variety of excellent restaurants— mostly expensive. Jervois Road and Herne Bay, in Upper Ponsonby, add to Ponsonby's culinary clout. The epicurean safari on Ponsonby Road follows ascending street numbers. Take your choice. How could you leave New Zealand without at least one first-rate game dish with the right wine? **Colin Brown's Gamekeeper**, 29 Ponsonby Rd., tel. 789-052 is one of the best choices. Stuffed calamari at **Franco's One on the Side**, 42A Ponsonby Rd., tel. 790-471; perhaps a very formal and expensive dinner under the chandeliers at **Orsini's**, 50 Ponsonby Road, tel. 764-563; an impeccably served meal of lamb fillets wrapped in spinach followed by a banana souffle or coffee marshmallow ice cream at **Wheelers**, 43 Ponsonby Road, tel. 763-185; a loin of lamb dinner outside on a summer night at the **Bronze Goat**, 108 Ponsonby Rd., tel. 768-193; lunch in **Oblio**'s garden conservatory, 110 Ponsonby Road, tel. 763-041; Sunday brunch and jazz at **Carthews**, 151 Ponsonby Rd.; a seafood dinner before an evening of partying at **Peppermint Park**, 161 Ponsonby Road, tel. 768-689; fish of the day immersed in the **Jungle Cafe**'s greenery, 222 Ponsonby Road, tel. 767-888; and last but not least, seafood chowder at **Fed Up**, 244 Ponsonby Road, tel. 768-469.

Believe it or not, Auckland has respectable French cuisine. Tony Astle's **Antoine's**, 333 Parnell Road, tel. 798-756, in an old restored house next to Parnell Village, serves excellent French food in very formal, traditional French colonial decor and atmosphere at an appropriately stiff price, NZ$110-$140 for two with wine. The international award-winning dishes of Warwick Brown's **Le Gourmet**, 1 Williamson Avenue, Ponsonby, tel. 769-499, are worthy of any major city and, not surprisingly, expensive. Other excellent splurge restaurants include: the **French Cafe,** 210B Court, Symonds St., tel. 771-911; **Hoffman's**, 70 Jervois Road, Herne Bay, tel. 762-049; **Delmonico's** in the Hotel de Brett, High St., tel 32-389, and Hyatt's **Top of the Town**, tel. 797-220.

Bagatelle, 279 Parnell Rd., tel. 396-289, one of Auckland's unsung heros of French Provincial cuisine, offers much more casual and less pricey French fare than Antoine's just down the street. Or try either of these outstanding French Provincial restaurants: **Anatole's**, 35 Cook St., tel. 534-3142, in the eastern suburbs or **Le Brie**, Chancery and Warspite Streets, tel. 733-935. Delicious fish, fowl, and fillet along with friendly service in any of these three restaurants comes to NZ$50-$60 for two, BYO (bring your own wine).

The search for Auckland's best fillet steak ends at **Harleys**, 25 Anzac Avenue, tel. 735-801. For stuffed venison roast and complementary ambience, visit **Le Rendezvous**, 473 Khyber Pass Road, Newmarket, tel. 540-903.

DAY 2
AROUND AUCKLAND

A full morning in Auckland covers the best viewpoints, parks
and museums, followed by lunch and a walking tour in the
Parnell District. Afterwards take a 1½ hour cruise in the Hauraki
Gulf. Return for brief downtown sightseeing before taking a
20-minute ferry ride to the North Shore for sunset sightseeing
and dinner. Return to Auckland by ferry in the late evening.

Suggested Schedule

7:00 a.m.	Early Breakfast.
8:00 a.m.	Catch a bus from the Downtown Bus Terminal to Cornwall Park and One Tree Hill or Mt. Eden Domain for easy walking and views.
10:30 a.m.	Tour the Auckland Domain, War Memorial Museum and Wintergardens possibly on an Auckland City Council guided walk.
12:00 noon	Lunch in Parnell.
1:30 p.m.	Mt. Cook Auckland Harbor cruise.
4:00 p.m.	Return to downtown and visit the Old Auckland Customhouse.
5:00 p.m.	Ferry to Devonport for a walk to sunset sightseeing at North Head and nearby Mt. Victoria.
6:30 p.m.	Dinner in Devonport at Rickerby's or Rocks Restaurant.
8:30 p.m.	Return to city by ferry.

Transportation

The Ferry Building Information Centre has all harbor information and timetables. The Devonport Ferry Service departs seven
days a week from the Queens Wharf, the terminal behind the
Ferry Building on Quay St., crossing the harbor in 20 minutes
to Devonport on the North Shore, for NZ$3.25 adult, NZ$1.65
child (round trip). The ferry leaves Queens Wharf every hour
on the hour, and leaves Devonport Wharf on the half-hour (until 11:30 p.m., Monday through Saturday). Captain Cook
Cruises, Ltd. (tel. 774-074), on Quay St., offers a variety of
cruises around the harbor: morning tea cruises, 9:45 to 11:30
a.m. (NZ$18); volcanic island cruise, 9:45 a.m. to 2:30 p.m.
(NZ$38); lunch cruise, noon to 2:15 p.m. (NZ$28); afternoon tea
cruise, 2:30 to 4:00 p.m. (NZ$18); an evening cruise, Monday to

Thursday, 6:45 to 9:15 p.m. (NZ$24); and a sunset cocktail
cruise, Friday, Saturday and Sunday, 6:00 to 8:00 p.m. (NZ$22).
Blue Boats (tel. 34-479) runs a ferry service between the North
Shore (Launch Steps next to Prince Wharf) and the city and also
conducts a one-hour harbor cruise for only NZ$5.

Sightseeing Highlights

▲▲▲**The Domain** is a beautiful park setting for the War
Memorial Museum, Wintergardens, Fern Glen, Planetarium and
Herb Garden. The Auckland City Council's (tel. 792-020) free
two-hour guided walk around the central city, featuring The
Domain, is an excellent introduction to the city.

▲▲▲**The War Memorial Museum**, on a grassy hilltop in
Auckland Domain, has outstanding views of Waitemata Harbour
and the North Shore. Even if you're not fond of museums, don't
miss its outstanding display of Maori and Pacific Island artifacts,
natural history exhibits covering the gamut of New Zealand's
flora and fauna, sea life, geology and paleontology, maritime
history exhibits, and a planetarium (Saturday and Sunday
shows). The Museum's "Centennial Street" is a reconstruction
of an Auckland shopping street of 1866. September to May,
open 10:00 a.m. to 5:00 p.m. (4:15 p.m. in winter), Monday
through Saturday, and Sunday 11:00 a.m. to 5:00 p.m.; June to
August, 10:00 a.m. to 4:15 p.m. Admission free.

▲▲ **Wintergardens** on the museum grounds in the Domain
holds over 10,000 South Pacific plants in a Cool House, and an
amazing variety of hothouse plants in the Tropical House and
the Fernery. Open 10:00 a.m. to 4:00 p.m.

▲▲**Mount Eden**, Auckland's highest point (643 feet), offers the
finest views over the city, surrounding water and the Waitakere
Ranges. Walk or drive up Mountain Road to the summit. This
volcano crater was used as an ancient Maori fortress, and
defense terraces and storage pits can still be seen around the
sides. Mount Eden is part of the Coast-to-Coast Walkway. It is
closer to the downtown than One Tree Hill. Seeing both Mt.
Eden and One Tree Hill requires a very early start. Catch a bus
from the Downtown Bus Terminal to either vantage point.

▲▲**One Tree Hill and Cornwall Park**—The terraced volcanic cone rises above Cornwall Park, which includes Acacia
Cottage, Auckland's oldest wooden building (1841). Walk or
drive past sheep-filled fields to the summit of what was once
the home of the region's largest Maori settlement.

▲▲▲**Hauraki Gulf**—Islands in the Hauraki Gulf Maritime
Park, extending from the Poor Knights Islands (see Day 4) to the
Alderman Islands off the Cormandel Peninsula, can be reached
by ferries, launches, yachts or seaplanes from Auckland's harborfront. Stop between 9:00 a.m. and 3:00 p.m. at the Hauraki

Gulf Maritime Park Information Centre, tel. 799-972, at the back of the Ferry Building for current time schedules and prices. There are about 100 islands out there, from the nearest, Rangitoto, an uninhabited volcano, to the furthest and largest, Great Barrier Island, covering 70,000 acres. Favorites include Rakino, Pakatoa, Mototapu, Waiheke, and Motuihe, with its excellent beaches and walks that draw thousands of people on summer days. Views from Waiheke's hilltop and the summit of Rangitoto are the best in the gulf. Walking up Rangitoto is well worth the effort. Wear sturdy footwear, sun lotion and sunglasses. Beach lovers, try Onetangi on Waiheke Island or Medlands Beach on Great Barrier Island.

▲**The Old Auckland Customhouse**, at the corner of Custom and Albert Streets near the harborfront, has been renovated in French Rennaisance-style into a shopping emporium with a restaurant, bar and cinema. See the downtown Auckland branch of the Clevedon Woolshed, with its great selection of knitwear, weaving, sheepskins, accessories and gifts.

▲▲**The Devonport Ferry** to the North Shore is one of the best ways to see Auckland from the water. The ferry service includes the *Kestrel*, built in 1905 and beautifully refurbished. Walk up to North Head for a good viewing point or up nearby Mt. Victoria (250 feet) for panoramic views. The ferries run until 11:00 p.m., Monday to Saturday, until 9:45 p.m. on Sunday.

Where to Eat
Take an evening ferry trip to Devonport for a stuffed leg of rabbit dinner and scrumptious desserts at **Rickerby's**, Fleet Street, Devonport, tel. 457-072. For reasonable seafood dishes with great harbor views in Devonport, try **Rocks**, 33 King Edward PDE, tel. 451-455. Also on the North Shore, **J.C.'s**, Beach Road, Rothesay Bay, tel. 478-8123, has superb dishes, decor and service. All three restaurants offer a great way to end a day of exploring nearby beaches and the harbor.

Itinerary Options
The **Coast-to-Coast Walkway** is marked by signs between the Waitemata Harbour on the east coast and the Manukau Harbour on the west. The Walkway connects Albert Park, Auckland University, Auckland Domain, Mt. Eden, One Tree Hill, and other points of interest, keeping to reserves wherever possible. At an easy pace, the eight-mile walk can be done in four hours, near bus routes all the way.

For those who desire a more leisurely walk, the Auckland City Council offers a series of free guided walks that take about 1½ hours each. **Albert Park** with its woods, daffodils, tropical glass house, cricket grounds and the remains of Albert Barracks,

built in the 1840s against Maori attacks, is located in the Auckland University grounds behind the main library. The **City Art
Gallery**, in a French Renaissance-style building at the southwest corner of Albert Park, houses the country's most complete
collection of New Zealand art, starting with early European settlement, as well as international and contemporary art. Open
from 10:00 a.m. to 4:30 p.m. on weekdays (6:30 p.m. on Friday)
and 1:00 to 5:30 p.m. on Saturday and Sunday. Admission free.

The **Museum of Transport and Technology**, commonly
referred to as MOTAT, on Great North Road in the Western
Springs District contains an interesting collection of everything
that buzzes, spins, calculates and moves, from music boxes and
vintage motor cars to steam locomotives. A whole building of
early flying machines features the remarkable inventions of
Richard Pearse, whose aircraft first flew in 1902—shades of the
Wright Brothers. The site's old buildings have been restored as a
pioneer village. An electric tram runs regularly between MOTAT
and the Auckland Zoo. Open daily from 9:00 a.m. to 5:00 p.m.,
weekends 10:00 a.m. to 5:00 p.m. Admission NZ$6 adult,
NZ$3 child.

For insatiable flying buffs, nearby **Keith Park Memorial
Airfield** houses a large collection of yesteryear's aircraft.

▲▲**Auckland Zoological Park**, next to MOTAT, offers a
chance to see kiwi birds in a special nocturnal house and the
tuatara (the only remaining link with the dinosaur), in addition
to a selection of over 1500 mammals, birds, reptiles and fish.
The zoo is mostly outdoors in spacious enclosures set in 45
acres of park-like gardens, with a children's zoo. Open daily
from 9:30 a.m. to 5:30 p.m., last admission 4:15 p.m. Admission, NZ$6 adult, NZ$3 child.

Hauraki Gulf Touring

A one-hour ferry ride (NZ$11 adult, NZ$5.50 child) to Waiheke
Island, Hauraki Gulf's largest and most central island, from Half
Moon Bay offers sample views of this maritime playground by
day and dusk. Flying (10 minutes, NZ$42 per person round-
trip) from Ardmore and Mechanics Bay "saves" over 1½ hours,
substituting flightseeing for the experience of a leisurely Gulf
boat ride. Waiheke's towns and beautiful white sand beaches are
an easy walk apart, so there really is no need for a car. The Royal
Forest and Bird Society's reserve at Onetangi, a bus ride from
the wharf, contains over two miles of bush walks. The **Charter
Cruise Company**, tel. 734-557, sails a 60-foot catamaran
around the harbor and inner gulf coast for two hours. Join in
the sailing activity or just watch the scenery. Adults NZ$25,
children NZ$8.50, with a lunch option for an additional
NZ$8.50. The **Volcanic Island Cruise**, tel. 774-074, departs

daily at 9:45 a.m. and 12:00 noon from Launchman's Steps for Rangitoto Island, NZ$44 adult and NZ$24 child, including a bus trip to the island's summit. **Blue Boats**, tel. 34-479, serve Rangitoto Island, Motutapu, Motuihe, and Rakino. The daily service departs Launchman's Steps Monday to Friday at 9:30 a.m., on Wednesday at 7:30 a.m. and 4:30 p.m., on Fridays at 6:00 p.m., and on weekends at 9:30 a.m. and 12:30 p.m. The ferries return Monday to Sunday at 3:00 p.m., on Wednesday at 10:30 a.m. and 6:15 p.m., and weekends at 5:45 p.m. Round-trip cost, NZ$8.50 adults, NZ$4.20 children. For solitude and lonely beaches, bush walks and a free campground, your only access to Great Barrier Island, 55 miles out, is by amphibian (**Sea Bee Air** for NZ$ 132 round-trip) or small plane. Several other airlines fly to the islands and offer flightseeing excursions.

Region Surrounding Auckland

Kiwi recreational life in Auckland revolves around water sports. They're either in or on the water. Most people seem to have boats or easy access to them. Little wonder with over 100 beaches within an hour's drive, dozens of offshore islands and their hundreds of sandy coves, 57 degrees the mid-winter average temperature and eight months of the year averaging in the high 60s and low 70s.

On the suburban shore north of Takapuna, see a chain of lovely beaches that runs from Castor Bay northward to Long Bay. The Wenderholm and Mahurangi Heads are special reserves with natural beauty and uncrowded shores. Starting at the city's downtown waterfront, the seven-mile scenic Tamaki Drive follows the south shore of Waitemata Harbour to St. Heliers Bay. Tamaki Drive, from Mission Beach, only 15 minutes from the downtown's waterfront, is a scenic road and bicycle route that passes through a series of beachfront suburban "villages," each with its own quiet character. Combine a trip down Tamaki Drive with a visit to either the **Bay Restaurant**, in Mission Bay, tel. 581-879, or **Lizzie's**, tel. 583-930, just down the street. Both have surprisingly sophisticated fare for a little eastern hamlet, such as superb seafood and salmon mousse, and charge accordingly. Both offer nice views of the Bay and Rangitoto Island and pleasant decor.

DAY 3
TOUR OF WAITAKERE RANGE AND NORTH SHORE

Spend the morning exploring the tracks and vistas of the
Waitakere Range and the black-sand beach at Piha along the
Tasman Sea. Then drive to the Henderson Valley's vineyards for
lunch and wine-tasting. In the afternoon follow the North
Shore's lovely beaches and bays to a dip in the Waiwera hot
springs before a farewell-to-Auckland dinner at one of Ponsonby Road's many restaurants.

Suggested Schedule

7:30 a.m.	After breakfast rent a car.
9:00 a.m.	Waitakere Range Scenic Drive.
11:00 a.m.	Piha or other black-sand beaches.
1:00 p.m.	Henderson Valley vineyards for lunch.
3:00 p.m.	Sightsee along North Shore beaches and bays.
4:30 p.m.	Enjoy Waiwera natural hot springs.
7:00 p.m.	Clean up and change for dinner.
8:30 p.m.	Dinner.

Driving to the Waitakere Range and Henderson Valley
Most major car rental companies operate in Auckland:
    Avis—22 Wakefield St., tel. 792-545, U.S. 800-331-2112
    Budget—26 Nelson St., tel. 734-949, U.S. 800-527-0700
    Hertz—154 Victoria St. W., tel. 34-924, U.S. 800-654-3131
Cars are expensive unless you have a discount voucher purchased as part of a package in the U.S. Beware of cut rates and
special deals for cars that may turn out to be problems. If you
rent a car, arrange to drop it off in Wellington without a penalty charge.
    From the downtown area, take Symonds Street over the
Route 1 Motorway to Dominion Road (Route 4) southwest to
Hillsborough Road (Route 15, which changes its name several
times), then westward to Titirangi Road (Route 24) which
becomes the Waitakere Scenic Drive. The Information Centre is
about three miles from the intersection of Routes 15 and 24 on
your left. About three miles past the Information Centre is the
turnoff (Piha Road) to Piha Beach. As you drive down this
secondary road, you'll see several tracks heading into the bush
to your right (north). This winding road covers about nine
miles and takes half an hour to Piha Beach.

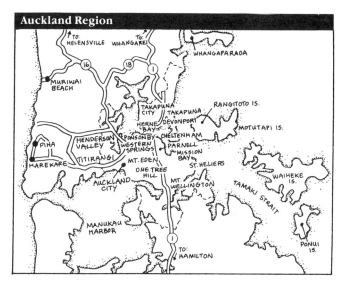

From the intersection of Piha Road and Scenic Drive, continue north on Scenic Drive for about another six miles to the intersection with Mountain Road on your right. Mountain Road will take you into Henderson Valley to the vineyards.

Driving from Henderson Valley to the North Shore, take Henderson Valley Road to Henderson. Turn right on Great North Road (Route 16) and then left on Te Atatu to Motorway 16 east through the downtown to Motorway 1, which crosses Waitemata Harbour to the North Shore. Exit at Takapuna-Devonport on Esmond Road (Route 26), turning left on the coastal road which heads north past the East Coast Bays (Milford, Castor Bay, Campbells Bay and others). At Long Bay, turn west briefly to the Old East Coast Road, which merges with Motorway 1 North just before Silverdale. Take Motorway 1 to Waiwera. Return to Auckland later on Motorway 1.

Sightseeing Highlights
▲▲▲**Waitakere Range Scenic Drive** within the Centennial Memorial Regional Park offers several spectacular views of Buckland and the Gulf, especially Pakinson's Lookout, Pukematekeo Lookout and View Road up to the summit of Mt. Atkinson. The Scenic Drive, a paved road running from Titirangi to Swanson via the Summit Ridge, passes through fine forests, with outlook views over the city and harbor. Stands of huge, ancient kauri trees remain along the walking tracks that thread through the thick bush. Fine specimens of kauri trees and

regeneration can be found at Titiranga and Piha Valley. The forest-covered hills of the Waitakere Ranges are threaded with walking tracks through bush thick enough to get lost in. ARA publishes a map of the Waitakere Ranges covering 135 walking tracks in the area. Public buses do not run to the Waitakere. For those not driving, catch a bus to Titirangi and be prepared to walk or hitchhike. The Aratakai Information Centre, tel. Turangi/TGN 7134, is on the Scenic Drive a couple of miles from Titirangi. It doesn't open until 1:00 p.m. on weekdays, 10:00 a.m. on weekends. The black-sand beaches of Muriwau, Piha, Karekare and the Tasman west coast are wild and treacherous favorites of surfers and gutsy swimmers. The Waitakere Ranges rise between the city and these west coast beaches. These beaches are accessible from trails winding down to the sand from the rim of mountains. Only swim in the rough surf near "life-savers" patrolling the beaches.

▲▲**Henderson Valley's vineyards**, on the lower slopes of the Waitakere Range in the western suburbs, produce some first-rate wines that can be tasted in pleasant outdoor restaurants. Almost a dozen wineries were established by Dalmatian settlers who came from Yugoslavia in the early 1900s to work in Northland's kauri gum fields.

▲▲**North Shore beaches and bays** stretch from Takapuna and Castor Bay to Long Bay, with East Coast Bays Cliff Walks providing wonderful views of the Hauraki Gulf islands.

▲**The Waiwera Hot Pools Leisure Resort**, tel. 42-65-369, about 30 miles north of Auckland adjoining the Waiwera Hotel, has public and private hot mineral pools, with varying temperatures, private saunas, suntan beds and sun lounges, and water slides for children. Open every day until late evening. Within walking distance of Waiwera, Wenderholm Regional Park offers an excellent combination day-trip of bush walking, hot pools and ocean swimming.

DAY 4
AUCKLAND TO THE BAY OF ISLANDS

The drive from Auckland to Russell in the Bay of Islands includes sidetrips to Kawau Island and scenic coastal areas south
and north of Whangarei. Take the Opua car ferry to Russell. The
day ends in Russell—known as the hellhole of the Pacific in the
early 1800s, first capital of New Zealand. Today, historic Russell
is an ideal touring base for the Bay of Islands Maritime and
Historic Park and its 150 islands.

Suggested Schedule	
7:00 a.m.	Breakfast, check out and departure from Auckland.
10:30 a.m.	Ferry from Sandspit to Kawau Island.
2:30 p.m.	Return to Sandspit and continue north to Mangawhai Heads and Tutukaka Coast.
5:30 p.m.	Opua car ferry to Russell.
6:00 p.m.	Arrive in Russell. Check in and head for the public bar at the Duke of Marlborough Hotel for refreshment and relaxation. If you're energetic, climb to the summit of Maki Hill for a great sunset view of the town and surroundings.
8:00 p.m.	Dine on the latest seafood catch at a restaurant on Russell's Strand. Sleep well in the Russell area.

Orientation
For touring purposes the Northland region can be divided into
four areas: the coast east of Highway 1 to the Bay of Islands; the
Bay of Islands northward to Doubtless Bay; Kaitaia and Cape Reinga; and the west coast from Aupori at the base of 90 Mile
Beach to Kaipara Harbour. The Northland Peninsula stretches
280 miles from Auckland to the tip of Cape Reinga. Including
lunch and rest stops, without sidetrips, it's a ten-hour drive
one-way. Russell in the Bay of Islands is no less than a five-hour
drive. With only three days in the Northland, concentrate your
sightseeing in the Bay of Islands region and on the west coast.
    The Bay of Islands is the birthplace of modern New Zealand's
history. The Treaty of Waitangi, establishing British rule, was
signed there on February 6, 1840. Fascinating links to the country's past will be found in Russell, on Waitangi Peninsula, and in

Kerikeri. Visit sites of conflict, struggle and habitation of Maoris, whalers, British soldiers and civil government, missionaries and early settlers, now embedded in tranquility and natural beauty.

The Bay of Islands consists of three resort areas: Paihai, the commercial, accommodations and excursions center; Russell, historic and fishing charter center; and Kerikeri, a scenic citrus-growing and historic center. Except for Paihia, a very popular Kiwi holiday resort area especially during Christmas and the January school holiday period, the region is not commercial and is protected by the Bay of Islands Maritime and Historic Park.

The Bay of Islands Maritime and Historic Park Headquarters (tel. 37-685) on the Strand in Russell should be the first stop, especially for anyone planning to cruise, sail, fish, hike or camp in the park. Upon arrival in Paihia, stop at the Public Relations Office on the waterfront.

On the Way to Russell and the Bay of Islands

Highway 1 up the east side of the Peninsula is the fastest route to the Bay of Islands. Highway 1 passes through rolling hill country with pastoral pockets of green flat land. At one time the entire region was covered by kauri, which has disappeared to be replaced by sheep and dairy livestock grazing. Virtually every town you'll see began as a timber town for cutting, milling or shipping kauri or for the digging of kauri gum. From 1853 to 1910, kauri gum was the second most valuable export from the region—after kauri timber.

The east coast is a constant variety of forms. The sandy crescents of Pakiri and Bream Bay are small safe harbors tucked into small bays between major peninsulas like Whangaparoa and Whangarei Heads, and the large deep-water inlet at Whangarei. On the drive north you'll pass Wenderholm Regional Park, where beautiful groves of trees on rolling hills are a backdrop to the beach. Pick up some fresh fruit at the fruit stalls of family orchards on the road to Warkworth before turning off to Sandspit for the ferry to Kawau Island.

Lovers of superb coastal scenery should follow the suggested schedule and take one or more detours: to Kawau Island from Sandspit (east of Warkworth); to Mangawhai Heads and the Mangawhai Walkway, and north through Waipu Cove (about 60 miles); through Whangarei to Whangarei Heads and Ocean Beach (about 22 miles); or along the Tutukaka Coast (about 48 miles), with access to great diving around the Poor Knights Islands.

Ferry Route - Bay of Islands

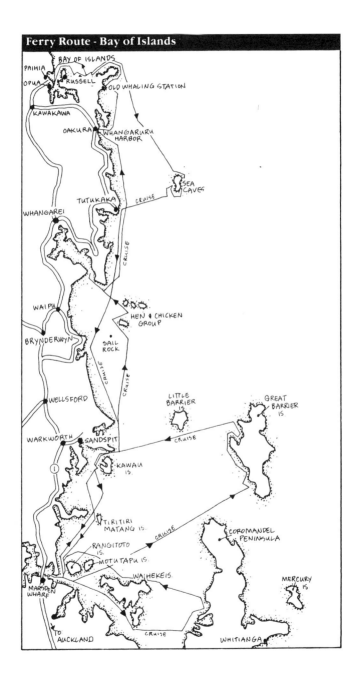

Transportation
The Northland is small enough to be covered by car in a few days, though for sailors, divers, deep-sea fishing and hiking enthusiasts it deserves at least a week. I prefer driving to the Northland for several reasons. It enables you to take several coastal sidetrips south and north of Whangarei. Bus services from the Bay of Islands to the west coast is infrequent, and without a car it is difficult to schedule visits to the Waipoua State Forest, Trounson Kauri Park, Kai-Iwi Lakes and Matakohe's museum. Bus transportation to the Coromandel Peninsula from Auckland runs infrequently and is difficult to time with the departure from Northland, although you could stay overnight in Auckland on Day 6 and head for Thames the next morning.

On the other hand, you really don't need a car in the Bay of Islands. Motorcoaches and buses connect Auckland with all major Northland attractions and the Bay of Islands with Dargaville. The NZRR runs daily coaches from Auckland, departing at 8:45 a.m. through Whangarei (noon arrival) to Paihia at 1:40 p.m., fare NZ$21 one-way. Newmans Coach Lines (205 Hobson St.) departs Auckland at 5:00 p.m. daily and 9:00 a.m. on Saturday, NZ$17 one-way.

Paihia, Russell, Waitangi and Kerikeri should be seen on foot. Minibuses can take you from Paihia to anywhere in the area. If you wind up on the wrong side of the water at night, it's an expensive mistake (how expensive depends on the number of people, time of night and season) but not fatal. Just call Bay Water Taxi (tel. 27-221) or Think Pink Water Taxi Service (tel. 27-161). A 15-minute ferry runs regularly between Paihia and Russell (NZ$3.25 adult round trip). Three miles south of Paihia, at Opua, a boat charter harbor, an inexpensive car ferry (car and two people one-way NZ$4.50) crosses the channel to Okiato Point, five miles from Russell. The last car ferry from Opua to Russell departs at 7:00 p.m. most nights except Friday, and later in the summer months.

Besides Russell's charm, Waitangi's historic sites, views and golf course and picturesque Kerikeri, enjoying the other sightseeing attractions in the Bay of Islands requires a launch cruise, boat charter or, as a last expensive resort, hiring a water taxi.

Sightseeing Highlights
▲▲**Kawau Island**, part of the Hauraki Gulf Maritime Park, is reached by ferry from Sandspit. Ferries (tel. 0846-8006) depart at 10:30 a.m. or noon, and return around 3:30 p.m., NZ$14 adult, NZ$7 child. Kawau Island was purchased (1862) and transformed into a subtropical delight of imported trees, plants and animals, including wallabies and kookaburras, by Sir George Grey, one of New Zealand's mid-19th century gover-

nors. The Governor's restored Mansion House and gardens are open daily from 9:30 a.m. to 3:30 p.m. Also see cottages and mineshafts (copper and manganese) dating from the 1830s.

▲**Mangawhai Cliffs Track**, a three-mile walkway near Mangawhai Heads, requires strong shoes for the rocky coast. The walk leads along cliff tops with magnificent seascape on one side and vistas of green hills on the other.

▲**Whangarei Falls** drop 75 feet into a green pool surrounded by luxuriant bush. With walkways above and below, it's a photographer's paradise. Visit the falls on the way to Tutukaka, taking Ngunguru Road.

▲▲▲**Bay of Islands Maritime and Historic Park** extends from Whangaroa Harbor to the north to Whangauru Harbor in the south, including 54 reserves of which 15 are offshore islands.

▲▲▲**Russell**, a wild whaling port (Kororareka) in the early 1800s, later a British settlement and scene of British-Maori conflict, today is a charming historic town. One of the first stops should be the Bay of Islands Maritime and Historic Park Headquarters on the waterfront, the Strand, for free information and informative audiovisual displays. The park ranger can tell you everything you want to know about hiking, fishing and camping and also issues camping permits. Along the waterfront, the Duke of Marlborough Hotel was one of Kororareka's most popular drinking spots, and holds New Zealand's customs house. At the southern end of the Strand stands the impressive Pompellier House, named after a Bishop (who didn't actually live there), open 10:00 a.m. to 12:30 p.m. and 1:30 p.m. to 4:30 p.m., NZ$2.75 adult and NZ$.70 child (tel. 37-861). The oldest surviving church in New Zealand, Christ Church, is nearby. The Captain Cook Memorial Museum, York St. (tel. 37-701), displays many relics of early town life and a 21-foot replica of Captain Cook's *Endeavor*. The museum is open daily from 10:00 a.m. to 4:00 p.m., NZ$1.65 adult and NZ$.20 child.

Right from the boat ramp end of the Strand, it's a 30-minute climb up historic Maki Hill (also known as Flagstaff Hill) for a panoramic view of the town and the Bay of Islands.

Where to Eat
En route to Russell from Auckland, if you're too hungry to drive any further, stop at **Ferryman's**, tel. 27-515, on the Opua ferry wharf for smoked marlin, or fresh local crayfish live from the tank. The setting, inside and outside, is perfect for seafood meals.

In Russell, the **Holiday Village Inn**, Chapel St., tel. 37-640, has a well-deserved reputation for big, delicious and inexpensive meals. Otherwise, the small group of local restaurants is much more expensive but offers the best food and selection in the Bay of Islands.

For some of the freshest fish you've ever tasted, heaps of shrimp cocktail or steak dishes, except on Sunday, try the **Reef Bar Bistro**, tel. 37-831, in the Duke Tavern. Next door, the **Duke of Marlborough** is very pricey dining in elegant surroundings, but their five-course lunch is a good value. **The Gables**, tel. 37-618, on the waterfront is moderately expensive but, with its very tasteful and comfortable early colonial decor, well worth a smoked marlin with avocado dinner preceded by creamy oyster or mussel chowder and topped off with their chocolate mocha mousse.

Where to Stay

If you plan to visit the Bay of Islands during peak summer months (December 15 through January) or school holidays, be sure to book well in advance through the Public Relations Office, P.O. Box 70, Paihia, tel. 27-426, open 8:30 a.m. to 5:30 p.m. Rates go up during these periods, too.

Wairoro Park, three fully equipped A-frame chalets and a cabin, about a mile from the Opua car ferry, on 160 acres in a beautiful setting on the shores of a cove, is highly recommended for families and groups, with rates starting at NZ$50 double, tel. 37-255. The **Arcadia Lodge**, Florence Avenue, tel. 37-756, with four attractive, comfortable, fully equipped and relatively inexpensive cabin units, also has great views of the Bay. Doubles start at NZ$36.

Russell Motor Camp, Longbeach Rd., tel. 37-826, has campsites (NZ$6 per night per person), caravan sites (NZ$5.50 per person) and cabins (NZ$30). **Brumby Farm Family Caravan Park**, tel. 37-704, on the Opua car ferry road has camping sites (NZ$8 minimum) and cabins (NZ$25). Campers should book at the Park Headquarters in Russell, take a water taxi and head for the beautiful Ranfurly Bay Reserve Park hut at the entrance to Whangaroa Harbour.

The **Motel Russell**, Matauwhi Bay Rd., tel. 37-854, has 13 very comfortable units, all with kitchens, in a wooded hillside location. Doubles start at NZ$50. New Zealand's first hotel, **The Duke of Marlborough**, The Strand, tel. 37-829, is cozy in an old-world way, well worth the NZ$70 rate for a double. The next best thing to staying overnight is joining the lively conversation at the Duke's pub or enjoying the fare in its fine dining room.

Alternative Accommodations

In the event that accommodations in Russell are full or not available in the right price range, here are some alternatives in

Paihia and Waitangi:

Backpackers will find a comfortable and clean place to stay for NZ$7 per person in four flats holding 36 persons at the **Centabay Travellers' Hostel**, Selwyn Road, tel. 27-466, for NZ$11 per person. **The Lodge**, Ivanhoe, Puketona Rd., tel. 27-466, also caters to backpackers with dorm-style accommodations at NZ$6. Secluded in a sheltered bay over a mile outside of Paihia toward Opua is **Smiths Holiday Camp**, tel. 27-678, with relatively inexpensive self-contained motel units at NZ$32 double and one room to deluxe cabins from NZ$20 double.

In the opposite direction, **Twin Pines Motor Camp**, Puketona Road, tel. 27-322, north of Paihia overlooking Haruru Falls, has caravan sites, cabins, hostels, and motel flats ranging from NZ$6 per adult to NZ$35 for two people. Almost four miles from Paihia past Haruru Falls, **The Lily Pond Holiday Park**, Puketona Road, tel. 27-646, offers some of the best deals in town for camping, caravan sites and 11 cabins, ranging from NZ$6 to NZ$25. **River Park Motor Camp**, tel. 27-525, along the Waitangi with a great view of Haruru Falls, is another excellent value for camping and caravaning at NZ$5.50 per person. The Mayfair Lodge, Puketona Rd., tel. 27-471, offers bunk-bed dormitory units for NZ$11 per person.

Ideal for families are the spotless, nicely furnished, reasonably priced units with every needed facility, service and amenity at the **Bay of Islands Motel**, Te Haumi, Tohitapu, Rd., tel. 27-348, the **Casa-Bella Motel**, McMurray Road, tel. 27-387, the **Aywon Motel**, Davis Crescent, tel. 27-684, and the **Ala-Moana Motel**, Marsden Rd., tel. 27-745, with singles from NZ$30-$48 and doubles NZ$42-$55. The **THC Waitangi**, tel. 27-411, on magnificent Waitangi Peninsula, costs about NZ$80 per day for two.

Itinerary Options

There's a one-way or round-trip cruise with marvelous coastal scenery from Auckland to Kawau Island, then on to Cape Brett and Russell in the Bay of Islands, and through the Bay of Islands Maritime and Historic Park to Whangaroa. Check on the Explorer cruise offered by the NZ Adventure Centre, costing $NZ175-$500 per person round-trip.

For those in a hurry, Mount Cook Airlines has three flights a day Monday to Saturday and one flight on Sunday to Kerikeri with a connecting motorcoach to Paihia. Sea Bee Air offers regular flights to Pahia.

The Clapham Clock Museum (tel. 71-384) on Water Street in Whangarei contains about 1000 varieties of clocks and watches.

Open Monday to Friday 10 a.m. to 4:00 p.m., 3:00 p.m. on weekends.

Tutukaka Coast is a favorite deep-sea fishing base. For all information, check at the Whangarei Deep Sea Anglers Club at the marina. The eight miles of coastline between Ngunguru and Sandy Bay are especially good for surfing. A short trail through the woods reaches splendid Whale Bay.

Poor Knights Islands, off the Tutukaka Coast, are world famous for diving and underwater photography. The subtropical waters in this area offer rich havens of colorful underwater life, with many school fish, large reef fish, and steep drop-offs covered in brilliantly colored anemones and sponges. The best time for scuba diving is January through May. October through December the visibility is poor. All necessary information, equipment and charters can be arranged with the Tutukaka Dive Shop or the Whangarei Deep Sea Anglers Club. From Tutukaka's marina, take a skin-diving or underwater photography trip to the Poor Knight Islands.

DAY 5

RUSSELL—BAY OF ISLANDS— WAITANGI—KERIKERI

Take a leisurely cruise from Russell to islands in the Bay of Islands Maritime and Historic Park. In the afternoon, leave Russell the same way you came, by the Opua Ferry, then drive through Paihai to historic Waitangi Peninsula. Visit the Treaty House and the nearby Maori meeting house and kauri war canoe. Drive to beautiful Haruru Falls on the way to Kerikeri. Explore Kerikeri Inlet until the sunset is gone and it's time for dinner at the Stone Store Restaurant.

Suggested Schedule

8:00 a.m.	Breakfast, local sightseeing and check out.
10:00 a.m.	Depart Russell on the Cream Trip.
12:00 noon	Picnic lunch at Otehei Bay on Urupukapuka Island.
1:30 p.m.	Return to Russell.
2:00 p.m.	Depart from Russell via the Opua car ferry and then drive through Paihia to the Waitangi Peninsula. Visit the Treaty House and other historic sites.
4:00 p.m.	Depart Waitangi and pass Haruru Falls on the way to Kerikeri. Check in upon arrival.
6:00 p.m.	Explore Kerikeri Inlet until sunset.
8:00 p.m.	Dinner at the Stone Store Restaurant, quiet relaxation and overnight in Kerikeri.

Sightseeing Highlights

▲▲▲**The Cream Trip** is one of the best ways, short of having your own cruiser or yacht, to see the Bay of Islands. It's named for a coastal launch route of the 1920s that collected cream and delivered mail and supplies to dairy farms. Fullers Cruises (tel. 27-421) operates the boat from Paihia (9:45 a.m. daily) and Russell (10:00 a.m. daily) to many islands, delivering mail and groceries to farmers and caretakers on Monday, Wednesday and Friday. The four-hour trip includes a lunch stop at Otehei Bay on Urupukapuka Island. Lunch and the cruise costs NZ$40. (Note: you can camp free almost anywhere on Urupukapuka Island and use the Cream Trip as your transportation to the island. Get the "Urupukapuka Island Campers" brochure at the park headquarters in Russell.) Fullers also has several other cruises.

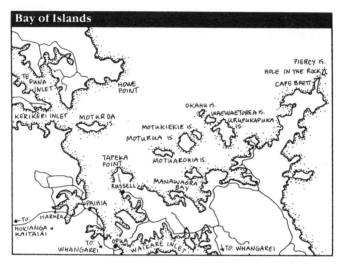

Bay of Islands

▲**Paihia** is jammed with motels and hotels, but the town center at the waterfront and wharf still has the character of a deep-sea fishing hub for dozens of local game-fishing boats. Look for crowds around the wharf as a sign that a magnificent game fish is being weighed in. The Fullers and Mt. Cook cruises, as well as most other sightseeing cruises and charters, leave from Pahai's wharf.

▲▲▲**The Waitangi National Reserve** on Waitangi Peninsula, only a mile from Paihia, is one of the most historic places in New Zealand. On February 6, 1840, the Treaty of Waitangi was signed on the lawn in front of the home of the first British Resident, James Busby. Local Maori chiefs, fearful of takeover of their land by France or other foreign countries, had asked for British protection. Over 2000 Maoris assembled there to meet Captain Hobson, who informed them that Queen Victoria would offer such protection under a treaty in return for ceding sovereignty to the Crown. With much opposition, which persists to this day, the treaty was signed and, on February 8, the British Colony of New Zealand was proclaimed with the hoisting of flags and a 21-gun salute. Nearby is the Waitangi Meeting House, a gift from the Maoris to New Zealand at the 1940 centennial, with wall carvings from many North Island tribes. Also nearby is a 118-foot Maori war canoe carved from kauri. The 18-hole Waitangi golf course is one of the finest and most scenic in New Zealand. Drive around it on the road that climbs nearly to the top of Mt. Bledisloe for the best panoramic views of the Bay of Islands.

On the way to Waitangi, stop off at the **Museum of Ship-wrecks**, a three-masted barque moored near the Waitangi-Pahia bridge holding a collection of diver Kelley Tarlton's salvage from local shipwrecks. Afterwards, walk or drive to **Haruru Falls**, a beautiful waterfall in a very lovely setting for a swim in the estuary of the Waitangi River surrounded by native trees. The falls, which are floodlit at night, can be reached by a 3.6-mile walking track through the Waitangi National Reserve or by driving less than two miles inland along the road to Puketona. The falls is also a beautiful spot for swimming in the estuary. While in the vicinity, consider having a snack lunch at the Dewdrop Bar or dining upstairs at Goffes Restaurant on the upper floor of Twin Pines Tavern (tel. 27-195).

▲▲**Kerikeri**, founded in 1819 as a mission station, today is known for its citrus fruit groves, large numbers of artists and craftsmen, and two historic buildings in lovely Kerikeri Basin—the Stone Store and Museum (1833), the oldest stone building in New Zealand, and Kemp House (1822), probably the oldest wooden building in the country. On the drive from Paihia to Kerikeri, the road is lined with orchards of oranges, mandarins, tangelos, kiwi fruit, tamarillos and feijoas, sheltered behind hedgerows in the landscape around Kerikeri. Approaching Kerikeri Basin, the red roof and white face of the Kemp House, set above the stolid Stone House on the shoreline, is a reminder that the "Fruitbowl of the North" is also a cradle of New Zealand's colonization. The most noteworthy and symbolic aspect of the Stone House is that it was built by missionaries to withstand native attacks that never occurred because of the humane and understanding way in which the missionaries involved themselves with the Maoris. Nearby is Rewi's Village, an accurate full-scale reconstruction of a Mauri *kainga* (unfortified village). A walking track follows the river from the Ranger Station to spectacular **Rainbow Falls**, about 90 feet high. For fun try the **Orchard Railway**, about half a mile of narrow track with a small train running through gum trees and subtropical orchards, ending at a restored country station.

Where to Stay
The **Kerikeri Youth Hostel**, Main Rd., tel. 79-391, on several acres just north of town, is within easy walking distance of river swimming and historic sites. Six dormitory rooms with 28 beds and a communal kitchen cost NZ$9 per person.

One of the prettiest sites for accommodations in the region belongs to the six chalet units of the **Riverview Chalets**, 28 Landing Rd., tel. 78-741, on the river bank overlooking Stone House and Kemp House, from NZ$55-$65 double. The **Spanish House Motel**, Inlet Rd., tel. 79-311, 2½ miles from town on 13 acres of farmland, with panoramic views of Kerikeri inlet, has NZ$45-$55 singles or doubles.

Where to Eat

Paihia has eating places of all sorts in proportion to its abundance of motels. The **Jolly Roger** on Kings Road, tel. 27-783, should take care of anyone's sit-down or take-away needs for shrimp, oysters, scallops and friendly service. Classic deep-fried dishes, local seafood and meat menu items are prepared in different styles downstairs and upstairs at the popular **Bella Vista** on the waterfront, tel. 27-451, at the French provincial-style **Courtyard Restaurant**, Beachhaven Motel, Marsden Road, tel. 27-444, and at the more expensive **La Scala**, Selwyn Road Shopping Center/upstairs, tel. 27-031.

For the famished traveler, I highly recommend the **THC Waitangi**'s, tel. 27-411, huge buffet lunch or Sunday brunch at the **Poolside Restaurant**. The grills and salads at the **Anchorage Grill** are plain and good. The hotel's **Governor's Room** is a budget-buster in the French tradition.

Jane's Restaurant, State Highway 10 between Paihia and Kerikeri, tel. 78-664, is a very cozy, relaxed place to have an early or late breakfast or a very good quality and moderately priced French provincial dinner, open seven nights a week. The tough competition in Kerikeri for Jane's is the BYO **Stone Store Restaurant**, tel. 78-194, located amid lawn and garden in the lovely Kerikeri Inlet, with an incredibly good, diverse and reasonably priced fish and meat menu.

Itinerary Options

Mt. Cook's Tiger Lily Cruises, tel. 27-099, Cape Brett Hole in the Rock Cruise departs Paihia at 9:30 a.m. and 1:00 p.m., returning at 12:30 and 4:00 p.m., and costs NZ$31 adult. The four-hour Super Cruise departs Paihia at 10:00 a.m. and returns at 2:00 p.m. The cruise visits Cape Brett, Piercy Island, Cathedral Cave and the Hole in the Rock at Cape Brett.

Join a skippered charter in Kerikeri for a day-trip along the Kerikeri Inlet into the Bay of Islands and up the coast to the Cavilli Islands and Whangaroa. High domed and craggy volcanic hills surround Whangaroa's harbor, dotted with small islands.

Golfers, check out the Kerikeri Golf Club, a championship course, with facilities available to visitors.

Scenic flightseeing charters are available at the Kerikeri Airport off Highway 10. The Bay of Islands Aero Club operates high-wing aircraft for good visibility and photography. Flights generally last from 20 minutes to two hours.

Bay of Islands: Cruising or yachting, perhaps combined with diving, game or light-tackle fishing, is the best way to experience the Bay of Islands for those with the time and budget. **Rainbow Yacht Charters** (Auckland: tel. 790-457; Opua: tel. 0885-27821; USA: 800-722-2288/Cal.: 800-277-5317) offers the most complete skippered or bareboat sailing holiday packages on a wide variety of yachts and motorcruisers. Cruising and sailing instruction is required for those without sufficient experience. Expect to spend from NZ$160 to NZ$800 per day, depending on the type of boat and season, and roughly double that for skippered boats. Five or six companions can bring down the per-person cost. The **Northland Charter Boat Association** in Russell and the **Game Fishing Charter Association** in the Pahia Marine Building offer fully-equipped single or shared charters, picking up people in Paihia, Russell or Waitangi at around 8:00 a.m., returning before 6:00 p.m.

Big game and sporting fishing are world class in the Bay of Islands. Zane Grey made them famous back in the 1920s. The main game fish are striped marlin, black and Pacific blue marlin, broadbill, mako, thresher, hammerhead and blue sharks, yellow fin tuna (New Zealand holds every world record), and yellowtail or kingfish. In December, striped marlin arrive and dozens of charter and private boats await with tackle and backup photography, smoking and trophy mounting services. The Bay of Islands International Billfish Tournament in early March and the Duke of Marlborough South Pacific Tournament in early May add festivities and fun to angling activities.

Diving in the sub-tropical waters of the Bay of Islands, around the Poor Knights Islands off the Tutukaka Coast or the Three Kings Islands off the northern tip of Cape Reinga, offers rich havens of colorful underwater life, with many school fish, large reef fish, and steep drops covered in brilliantly colored anemones and sponges. Some of the best diving areas are: Cathedral Cove almost splitting Piercy Island; between Howe Point and Cape Wiwiki on the Purera Peninsula east of Kerikeri; around Dog Island; Bird Rock and Twins Rock; Hope Reef in the Albert Channel off of Unupukapuka; Paramena Reef in Te Uenga Bay; Whale Rock northwest of Okahu Island; Waewaetorea, Takarota Rock between Motutakapu and Nakataunga, and Tokananohia Reef. A seven-hour dive trip with **Pahia Dive and Fishing Trips**, including all equipment, costs about NZ$100 per person.

DAY 6

WEST OF THE BAY OF ISLANDS—SOUTH TO COROMANDEL PENINSULA

Leave the Bay of Islands heading for the west coast of Northland, then south to visit the Waipoua Kauri Sanctuary on the way to Dargaville. Visit two exceptional regional museums, in Dargaville and Matakoke, before continuing south past Auckland to Thames on Coromandel Peninsula.

Suggested Schedule

7:00 a.m.	Breakfast in Kerikeri.
8:00 a.m.	Depart for west coast.
11:00 a.m.	Waipoua Kauri Sanctuary.
12:30 p.m.	Picnic lunch on the West Coast Beach adjoining Dargaville.
1:30 p.m.	Visit Dargaville regional museum.
3:00 p.m.	Otamatea Kauri and Pioneer Museum in Matakoke.
4:00 p.m.	Leave for final leg of trip to Coromandel Peninsula.
8:30 p.m.	Arrive in Thames, Coromandel Peninsula.
9:00 p.m.	Late dinner and a waterfront stroll before retiring.

Driving to the West Coast, Auckland and Thames
Head west from Kerikeri on Highway 12 to Opononi via Rawene (about 1½ hours drive). From there, continuing on Highway 12 through the Waipoua Kauri Forest and by Trouson Kauri Park to Dargaville, is less than a two-hour drive without stops. Follow Highway 12 through Matakoke to Highway 1 south. Dargaville to Highway 1 also is less than two hours; allow about a half an hour at the Dargaville Museum and about 45 minutes at the museum in Matakoke. From Wellsford on Highway 1 it's 1½ hours to Auckland. You should pass by Auckland at about 6:00 p.m. It's about an hour on Highway 1 from Auckland to just before Pokeno, where you turn east for another hour on Highway 2 to Kopu, a few miles south of Thames. Turn north on Route 26 to Thames.

Sightseeing Highlights
▲▲▲The Waipoua Kauri Forest contains some of the best specimens of the North Island's once vast forests of giant kauri

trees. The Northland's early history was very much shaped by the presence of these aged giants, first cut at a frenzied pace for local use and export as ship's masts and building material. Then the resinous kauri gum was dug from the ground by thousands of Yugoslavian diggers for export to the United States and Europe to make varnish. In just a few decades of the early 19th century, kauri forests were reduced to small scattered stands. Rivaling California redwoods in height (170 ft.), girth (50 ft.) and age (some as old as 2000 years), kauris can be seen in two forests east of Highway 12 north of Dargaville: **Waipoua Forest Sanctuary** and **Trounson Kauri Park**, located about nine miles south of Waipoua (including a few campsites). The Waipoua Forestry Headquarters (tel. Donnellys Crossing 605) is on Highway 12 on the southern end of the forest. Other kauri preserves can be seen in the Omahuta Kauri Forest in the Ngaiotonga Scenic Reserve east of Russell, the Puketi Forest northwest of Kerikeri, the Waitakere Ranges, and on Coromandel Peninsula.

▲▲**Regional museums** at Dargaville and Matakoke, as well as Russell and Kaitaia, contain extensive material on the "Kauri Era." The **Otamatea Kauri and Pioneer Museum** (tel. 37-417) in Matakoke has a unique kauri gum collection and the kauri gum story is told with photographs, models, early furniture, industrial tools and more. Open daily 9:00 a.m. to 5:00 p.m.

▲**Dargaville**, a thriving port during the kauri timber and gum era, has the **Northern Wairoa Maori, Maritime and Pioneer Museum** housing pre-European Maori, kauri and maritime sections. Open daily, except Saturday, 2:00 to 4:00 p.m. only. West of Dargaville, stretching from Kaipara Head north to Maunganui Bluffs, is the Northland's longest ocean beach (68 miles), the West Coast Beach, with black iron sand typical of Tasman Sea beaches.

Where to Stay

There is a good choice of motor camps in the Thames area, including **Dickson Park Motor Camp**, Victoria St., Teraru, tel. 87-308, **Boomerang Motor Camp**, Coromandel Rd., Te Puru, tel. 78-879, and **Waiomu Bay Motor Camp**, Highway 25, tel. Te Puru 78-777. North of Coromandel are the **Angler's Lodge and Motor Park**, **Coromandel Motel & Caravan Park**, and the **Oamaru Park Tourist Flats and Caravan Park**, all offering caravan sites, on-site vans, tourist cabins and in some instances tourist flats and motel units.

There are five hotels in Thames—the **Brian Boru Hotel**, Pollen St., tel. 86-523, **Imperial**, 476 Pollen St., tel. 86-200, **Junction Hotel**, Pollen St., tel. 86-908, **Salutation Hotel**, 400 Mary St., tel. 86-488, and **Warwick Arms**, Pollen St., tel.

86-183. They range in price from NZ$20 to NZ$40 singles and doubles. The **Brian Boru**, built in 1868, is the most exceptional (and expensive), especially its two-day Agatha Christie Weekends, which combine rafting, a beach trip, wine tasting, two-nights lodgings, sumptuous breakfasts, supper and buffet dinner, and a fun "whodonit" involving 30 guests and eight actors, for NZ$300 per person.

The Thames area has about a dozen very good small motels that offer most amenities including kitchens for NZ$35-$55 per night single. The **Puru Park Motel**, Puru Bay, tel. 84-378, is the top of the group. The **Motel Rendezvous**, Highway 25 at Kopu, tel. 88-536, at NZ$32 single is the most reasonable.

Where to Eat
In Thames, the **Brian Boru Hotel**, tel. 86-523, serves excellent bistro lunches and Sunday night smorgasbord, 5:00 to 8:00 p.m.

Except for the Brian Boru, save your dining money for the Aorangi Peak or Rumours in Rotorua on the evening of Day 7 or on Day 8. Check on Pollen St. in Thames for a variety of eateries. The **Hotel Imperial** will do nicely for reasonably tasty and moderately priced counter meals and more expensive (but not outstanding) cuisine in the **Regency Room**. Down the street, the **Pizza Cabin**, 702 Pollen St., is not what you think with its diverse and inexpensive menu ranging from pizza to delicious Bluff Oysters, steak and other dishes.

The **Bakehouse** on Wharf Road in Coromandel, with its delicious bread and baked goods, is an excellent place to pick up ingredients for a picnic lunch tomorrow.

Itinerary Options
Kai-Iwi Lakes, three relatively unspoiled lakes about 19 miles north of Dargaville, deserve a side-trip on the way south to Dargaville for trout fishing, swimming and tramping. From Highway 12 at Maropui, turn west on Omamari Road to the end, then right onto Kai-Iwi Lakes Road, then right on Domain Road to Taharoa Domain. The white sand beach on this beautiful lake is a perfect stop for swimming or fishing before continuing to Auckland and Cormandel. Taharoa Domain also offers lakeside camping.

DAY 7
COROMANDEL PENINSULA—ROTORUA

Make a partial circuit of the west and east Coromandel Peninsula coastlines, then follow the Bay of Plenty through Tauranga and Mt. Maunganui before turning south to the Rotorua lake and thermal region.

Suggested Schedule

8:00 a.m.	After breakfast, head north to Coromandel.
10:00 a.m.	Visit Coromandel.
12:00 noon	Take Highway 309 to the east coast for a picnic lunch on Hot Water Beach.
1:30 p.m.	Head south to Tauranga on the Bay of Plenty.
5:00 p.m.	Arrival in Tauranga and possible side trip to Mount Maunganui.
8:30 p.m.	Arrive in Rotorua, check in and enjoy a thermal bath before a late dinner.

Driving from Coromandel to Rotorua
Just 75 miles southeast of Auckland, the Coromandel Peninsula's volcanic mountains and rugged coastal scenery jut out between the Hauraki Gulf and the Bay of Plenty. A car is necessary on the Peninsula. The Auckland Railways Road Service's coaches travel between Auckland and Thames, but otherwise bus service is limited to Thames, Coromandel and Whitianga on the Bay of Plenty.

Leaving Auckland on Highways 1 and then 2, the drive along connecting Highway 25 is lush and scenic. The route passes through rolling green farmland with few settlements. Just a few miles past Mangatawhiri, the road branches to the left toward the extensive vineyards of Mangatangi. The pine forest south of Highway 2, planted by the New Zealand government, can be used for recreation. Route 25 from Thames to Coromandel is paved, as is Route 25 from Whitianga south to the Bay of Plenty. Otherwise, most of the roads on the Peninsula are loose gravel and slow going. Take Highway 25 from Thames to Coromandel along the Firth of Thames, then backtrack three miles to Highway 309, an unpaved winding road with spectacular views. Continue south through Coroglen for about ten miles watching for the turnoff to Hot Water Beach. A fork in the road to Hot Water Beach leads to Hahei Beach.

After a beach stop, continue south on Highway 25 to Waihi

Coromandel Peninsula

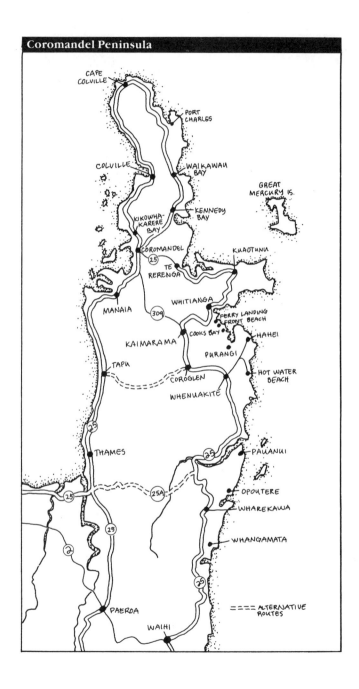

where it connects with Highway 2 south to Tauranga, Mt.
Maunganui and the turnoff to Highway 33 to Rotorua which is a
few miles past Te Puke. Highway 33 merges with Highway 30
into Rotorua.

Orientation
Coromandel Peninsula is a nature lover's and sportsman's
paradise, sprinkled with reminders of the area's gold mining
and kauri milling days. Coastal roads follow a wonderfully
varied coastline, with side roads leading to some of New
Zealand's most scenic beaches. The forested Coromandel
Range is cut through by winding mountain and valley roads
connecting west and east coasts that offer several trip options,
such as the Kauaeranga Valley Road, the Tapu-Coroglen Road
and Highway 309. Mayor Island off the southwest coast is the
center of deep-sea fishing activity. You'll arrive too late to visit
the Thames Information and PR Centre (Queen St., tel. 87-
284). It's the first place to go in the morning for information
and maps.

Sightseeing Highlights
▲**Coromandel's Courthouse**, built in 1873 for the gold
warden 20 years after discovery in Coromandel of the first gold
in New Zealand, now serves as the local Council Chambers.

▲▲**Highway 309**, a narrow and winding unpaved "short-cut"
across the peninsula from Coromandel Harbour to Kaimarama,
has stunning scenery.

▲▲**Mercury Bay to Waihi Beach** displays spectacular headland and beach scenery, though it can be very crowded during
vacation and holiday periods. In this coastal stretch, stop off at
Hahai Beach, Hot Water Beach, Pauanui and Mount Paka. At
Opou, a turnoff to the left south of Hikuai, the Opoutere Youth
Hostel (tel. Whangamata 59-072) puts you within a short walk
of Opoutere Beach.

▲▲**Hahei Beach** (pink sand) and **Hot Water Beach** are
beautiful beaches, quite different from one another. Within a
few hours of low tide, just dig a hole on Hot Water Beach between the cliff and large rock offshore to soak in your own
natural hot pool bath seeping through the sand. The fabulous
headland scenery, two *pa* (Maori village) sites, nearby blow
holes (seawater forced through holes in coastal rocks) at the
southern end of Hahei's pink sands and the huge cavern at
Cathedral Cove Reserve on the northern end make this an unsurpassed beach getaway. Tent sites are available at Hahei
Tourist Park, in case you just can't leave.

▲**Pauanui** holiday town nestles in the pines along a golden
beach.

▲Twin-peaked **Mount Paka** across the Tairua Harbour from Pauanui is the site of an old *pa*, where still-visible earthworks rise up from the sea over 500 feet.

▲▲**The Bay of Plenty**—There are plenty of attractions to keep you in the Bay of Plenty on the way to Rotorua: mild climate, fine broad beaches, clear water, excellent game-fishing or diving near Mayor Island, and great bush walks on the island, Tauranga's beautiful parks, "The Mount" with its magnificent views, natural hot saltwater pools, a wonderful surf beach (Ocean Beach) and excellent white-water rafting.

▲**Mount Maunganui**—This beach resort, reached by ferry on the eastern shore of Tauranga's Harbor, has a 760-foot wooded peak that is worth the climb for outstanding views of the ocean, Matakana Island, Tauranga City and Harbour, and the surf beach stretching for 12 miles south to Maketu's headland.

Where to Stay

The best values in Rotorua are: the dormitory rooms at the **YHA Hostel**, Eruera and Hinemary Streets, tel. 476-810, at NZ$11 per person; the serviced rooms and cabins for NZ$8-$12 at the **Ivanhoe Tourist Lodge**, 54 Haupapa St., tel. 86-985; and the **Waiteti Holiday Park**, 14 Okona Crescent, Ngongotaha, tel. 74-749, for a variety of tent sites, caravan sites, bunkhouse beds, tourist cabins and flats, all in a wooded river-bank setting (with trout), at NZ$11-$32 double. With its charming and well-equipped cabins, **Rainbow & Fairy Springs**, State Highway, tel. 581-887, is a perfect place for families of any size to relax in a pretty setting outside of town. Rates per cabin range from NZ$15 to NZ$45. Less charming but cheaper are the **Cosy Cottage**, tel. 83-793, cabins, starting at NZ$15 for two, and the **Rotorua Thermal Motor Camp**, Old Taupo Rd., tel. 86-385, starting at NZ$22 double.

Couples hunting for homey, attractive, clean, friendly, and comparatively inexpensive B&Bs with their own mineral pools should book in advance at either **Morihana Guest House**, 20 Toko St., tel. 88-511, or **Tresco Guest House**, 3 Toko St., tel. 89-611, for around NZ$25 per person or NZ$34-$38 per couple.

There are plenty of less expensive (NZ$28-$50) twin or double motel flats in Rotorua, such as the **Motel McHale**, 281 Fenton St., tel. 89-612, **Mayfair Motel Flats**, 7 Arawa St., tel. 80-436, and the **Victoria Motel**, 10 Victoria St., tel. 84-039.

If you are looking for total comfort, service, all facilities (freshwater, thermal/mineral and spa pools) and lovely grounds, expect to pay upwards of NZ$50 double at, for example, the **Fernleaf Motel**, 23 Toko St., tel. 87-129, or the **South Pacific Motel**, 98 Lake Rd., tel. 80-153.

The **THC Rotorua International**, Whakarewarewa, tel.

81-189, and the **Sheraton Rotorua**, Fenton St., tel. 81-139, share honors for the premier address in Rotorua. The latter has the edge for luxury accommodations, exterior and interior design and decor, and health and fitness facilities. Both hotels start at about NZ$140 for double rooms, which in U.S. dollars is not bad for what you get.

Where to Eat

First priority for dining (or should I say feasting) in Rotorua goes to a traditional Maori *hangi*. The carefully timed and controlled steam oven cooking of lamb, pork, seafood, vegetables, pumpkin and pudding has been perfected by large hotels like the **Rotorua International**, tel. 81-189, the **Rotorua Travelodge**, tel. 81-174, the **Tudor Towers Restaurant**, tel. 81-285, in Government Gardens, and **Geyserland Motor Hotel**.

Start your quest for good food, light meals, grills or counter service on Arawa Street with fish and steaks at the upstairs **Palace Tavern and Friar Tuck**, tel. 81-492, in Ye Olde English Tavern atmosphere; perhaps *coq au vin* at the French provincial bistro, **Gormet**, tel. 82-198; and, for pancake fans, the **Pancake Parlour Restaurant**. Tutanekai Street has a few local and tourist favorites : for game dishes, the enormous portions at **Karl's Dining Room**, tel. 80-231; roast beef and lamb, seafood and wild game at **The Bushman's Hut**, tel. 83-285; a superb fixed-price lunch at the **Gazebo**, tel. 81-911.

Cobb & Co., tel. 82-089, in the Grand Establishment on Hinemoa Street, is reliable, from decor to relatively inexpensive and satisfying food, seven-day-a-week service from 7:30 a.m. to 10:00 p.m.

If you're going to Ohinemutu Village, make reservations at the **Lake Tavern Restaurant**, tel. 85-585, in a great old building overlooking the lake. When visiting the Agrodome, don't miss the **Agrodome Tea Room** for a savory lunch and excellent deserts. Sunday smorgasbord (6:00 p.m. to 9:00 p.m.) at the **Geyserland Hotel** while watching Whaka's thermal activity is a special treat. The literal translation of Whakarewarewa is "to rise-up," originally referring to the uprising of a local Maori war party; today the name refers to steam clouds gushing skyward at unpredictable intervals. A dining highlight in Rotorua is **Aorangi Peak**, tel. 86-957 (book ahead!), over 1000 feet up Mt. Ngongotaha. If the view and the venison medallions don't leave you breathless, the bill will. Otherwise, trek up to dance on Friday or Saturday night and enjoy the cocktail bar.

Less expensive, without a mountaintop view but with better cuisine and desserts, is **Rumours**, tel. 477-277, at 581 Pukuatua. Like Aorangi Peak, you may have to make reservations even before leaving Auckland.

DAY 8
ROTORUA—LAKE TAUPO

The region between Rotorua and Lake Taupo is crammed with so many things to see and do that visiting the best of it takes a full day and is worth every minute of it. The day starts early with stops at trout springs just outside of Rotorua and thermal, Maori and other attractions in Rotorua. Move south after lunch through thermal and Waikato Valley sightseeing to Lake Taupo. Before the day is over you'll have seen hot water springs, eerie boiling mud pools, steaming silica terraces, the blue-green lake of Waimangu Cauldron, smoldering rocks, steaming bush and cliffs with hot water gurgling out of rock crevices.

Suggested Schedule	
7:00 a.m.	Rise early for a full day.
8:00 a.m.	Breakfast and check out.
9:00 a.m.	Rainbow and Fairy Springs.
10:30 a.m.	Whakarewarewa and the Maori Arts and Crafts Institute.
12:00 noon	Snack lunch at the Agrodome.
1:00 p.m.	Waimangu Thermal Valley.
3:30 p.m.	Huka Falls, Aratiatia Rapids and the Wairakei Geothermal Steam Power Station.
6:00 p.m.	Check in at Taupo accommodations and fish for trout in Lake Taupo while there's still light.
8:00 p.m.	Dinner followed by a lakefront stroll.

Orientation
Ancestors of the Maoris landed on the shores of the Bay of Plenty around 1340 AD and pushed inland to Lake Rotorua, the center of a giant (150 miles long and 20 miles wide) thermal region. The natural wonders confirmed the phenomenal activities of the gods. The many lakes and thermal activity supplied food and warmth. The result today is New Zealand's largest concentration of Maori culture, arts and crafts, in the midst of an extraordinary assortment of thermal sites, volcanic mountains and the world's best trout fishing.

To the south of Rotorua, the beautiful Waikato River flows placidly northward, with a brief intermission at Huka Falls. To the east of Rotorua is a collection of magnificent bush-fringed lakes and the Bay of Plenty, which is about the same distance from Rotorua as Lake Taupo to the south. The Bay of Plenty's waters teem with yellow fin and mako shark. Fine beaches abound.

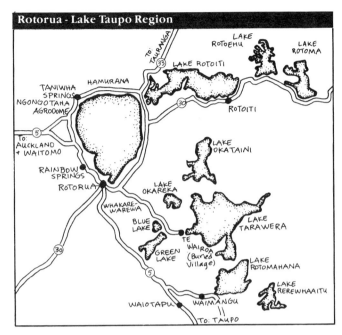

Rotorua - Lake Taupo Region

Sightseeing Highlights

▲▲▲**Rotorua** is "Spa City," with over 600,000 visitors annually. The resort hugs the southwestern shore of Lake Rotorua. The city's three primary attractions are Whakarewarewa Thermal Reserve, Maori Arts and Crafts Institute, and Government Gardens.

▲▲▲**Whakarewarewa Thermal Reserve** is the best location in New Zealand to see many of the elements of living Maori culture. Walk around the traditional village site, Whakarewarewa, where carved meeting houses (*maraes*) and huts are located among boiling pools and geysers. The local Maoris still use thermal energy for cooking, washing and heating. The Whakarewarewa thermal area is entered through a replica of a fortified Maori village (*pa*) and ornately carved gateway. Steaming cracks, boiling mud, silica terraces and small geysers lead to Pohutu Geyser, New Zealand's highest (100 ft.), with erratic bursts of boiling water and steam clouds. Open daily from 8:30 a.m. to 4:30 p.m.

▲▲▲**The New Zealand Maori Arts and Crafts Institute**, outside the main entrance to the Whakarewarewa, is the training center for Maori wood carvers. Maori flax weaving techniques are demonstrated there as well. Open 8:30 a.m. to 4:30 p.m.

▲▲**Government Gardens** and its Elizabethan-style **Tudor Towers**, built as a bath house in 1906-7 and restored by the city, houses the Rotorua Museum and Art Gallery, the Fleur International Orchid Gardens, the Rotorua Cricket Club, The Sportsdrome (a new sports center), Polynesian Pools and thermal waters of varying mineral content and temperature. Pool hours are 9:00 a.m. to 10:00 p.m., NZ$5.50 per person.

▲▲**Rainbow and Fairy Springs** (tel. 81-887) combine beautiful bush growth, pools full of rainbow and brown trout viewed above and below water, and a variety of other attractions. Open 8:00 a.m. to 5:00 p.m. To see more trout pools in equally beautiful settings, continue north on Highway 5 to Taniwha Springs and Hamurana Springs.

▲**The Agrodome** (tel. 74-350), seven miles from Rotorua, offers three shows daily (9:15 a.m., 11:00 a.m. and 2:30 p.m.) with a 60-minute demonstration of sheep shearing and the use of sheep dogs. Combine the show with lunch at the Agrodome Tea Room. NZ$3.50 per person.

▲▲**Ohinemutu** is an unusual Maori village with both the Tamatekapua Meeting House and Tudor-style Maori Anglican St. Faith's Church (with Maori carvings). The two structures have faced each other for generations next to Lake Rotorua. There are Maori concerts every night in summer at the Ohinemutu meeting house (8:00 p.m., tel. 82-269).

▲▲**Ngongotaha**, three miles west on Highway 5, has natural pools filled with thousands of rainbow, brown and brook trout amidst 30 acres of natural growth, including Rainbow and Fairy Springs, a bird aviary, nocturnal kiwis and a deer farm. Drive up Mount Ngongotaha to the Aorangi Peak Restaurant for a breathtaking panorama.

▲▲▲**Maori hangi**, a Polynesian feast traditionally steam-cooked in an underground pit, includes chicken, pork, seafood, fish and other basics and delicacies and, after dinner, a Maori concert. *Hangis* are put on at several hotels around town for about NZ$18 per person. The THC International Hotel traditionally has had the best one.

En Route to Taupo

Taupo is a 1½ hour (50-mile) drive from Rotorua on Highway 1. About 12 miles from Taupo, shortly before Wairakei, is the turn-off to Aratiatia Rapids and Huka Falls. Wakirakei means "Waters of Adorning," an apt name for this geothermal area. Huka means "foaming" which also describes the sight of the blue-green Waikato River plunging through a narrow cleft of rock.

▲▲**Huka Falls** is not high, but the Waikato River funneling powerfully through a narrow gorge near Taupo catapults the water over the ledge into the calm pool below.

▲▲▲**Aratiatia Rapids** are about two miles from Highway 5, just north of its intersection with Highway 1. The rapids flow through a deep, rocky ravine to a small spillway and hydro-electric power station at the head of the rapids on the Waikato River downstream from Lake Taupo. Millions of native plants have been planted in the area around the rapids. Water is released over the dam from 10:00 to 11:30 a.m. and 2:30 to 4:00 p.m. daily.

▲▲▲**Waimangu Thermal Valley** contains Waimangu Cauldron, one of the world's largest boiling lakes. Walk past the bubbling crater lake to the shores of Lake Rotomahana, where a launch takes you to the Steaming Cliffs and site of the former Pink and White Terraces. The devastating eruption of Mount Tarawara, on June 10, 1886, is said to have been foretold by the appearance of a phantom war canoe paddling across Lake Tarawara ten days before the eruption. Several villages were completely destroyed, including Te Wairo, a busy center for trips to the world famous Pink and White Terraces of Lake Rotomahana. The three truncated peaks of Mt. Tarawara, across Lake Tarawara, a short distance from Te Wairo, are still devoid of vegetation, an ominous reminder of the disaster that occurred only a moment ago in geological time. Visit the buried village of Te Wairoa, Blue and Green Lakes and the Waiotapu thermal area containing the Lady Knox Geyser that erupts daily at 10:15 a.m. to a height of 60 feet. See the Bridal Veil Falls cascade over tinted silica terraces changing colors from white through deep red and lemon to emerald green. NZ$5.50 adult, NZ $2.50 child, with an extra charge of NZ$5 (NZ$3/child) for the launch ride. This tour is covered by a full-day's NZRR excursion for NZ$24.

▲**The Wairakei Geothermal Steam Power Station**, 50 miles south of Rotorua between Huka Falls and the Aratiatia rapids, generates billows of clouds over an interesting energy project. Take the walkway from Huka Falls to Aratiatia through wildflowers in season.

▲▲**Lake Taupo** fills a gigantic (238 square mile) crater. One of the biggest volcanic eruptions in history, greater than Karakatoa and Mt. St. Helens combined, devastated the region 1800 years ago. Today Lake Taupo is the trout fishing capital of the world. About 100 years ago, trout eggs were brought from California to what turned out to be perfect breeding grounds at Lake Taupo. Fishing in the sparkling clear lake waters, at the mouths of streams flowing into the lake from the Kaimanawa Mountains or in the trout-pools of the famed glacier-fed Tongariro River yields legendary rainbow (3-6 lbs.) and brown trout (5 lbs. and over) from April to August during spawning runs. Lake Taupo also offers superb water-skiing, pleasure boating and swimming.

Where to Stay

Thanks to thousands of beds in the Taupo area, many in very decent, inexpensive motel flats and two- to five-berth furnished cabins, even hoards of fisherman at holiday times shouldn't cause a serious problem. The Public Relations Office, tel. 89-002, near the lakefront, can take care of your accommodation and other needs. For around NZ$16-$22 per night for two persons, the **Acacia Holiday Park**, Acacia Bay Road, tel. 85-159, the **Waitahanui**, tel. 87-183, and **Taupo Cabins**, 50 Tonga St., tel. 84-346, are sure winners.

The next level of accommodation is motel flats in the NZ$35-$45 range for doubles: **Acapulco**, tel. 87-174, **Dunrovin Motel**, 140 Heuheu St., tel. 87-384, and **Motel Taupo**, Four Mile Bay, tel. 85-992. The local PRO knows many others.

There are many more good choices for NZ$40-60 double: **Adelphi Motel**, Heuheu St., tel. 87-594, **Birchlands Motel**, 120 Robert St., tel. 88-569, **Continental Motel**, 9 Scannell St., tel. 88-398, **De Brett Thermal Motel**, Napier Highway, tel. 87-080, **Guestward Ho Motel**, 9 Tui St., tel. 87-487, **Lynwood Lodge**, tel. 84-967, **Motel Trianon**, 63 Mere Rd., tel. 84-222, **Shoreline Motel**, Waitahanui, tel. 86-912, and many other relatively new ones.

Where to Eat

Taupo is not a fancy resort, but large numbers of vacationers year-round from around the world, who come for spectacular lake fishing and views, have assured quality eating, from tea room snacks and light lunches at the **El Toreador Coffee Lounge** and the **Alpine Coffee Lounge** on Horomatangi Street to the extravagantly expensive and superb **Milly's** (Lane Cover Motel) and Huka Lodge (see below).

Great lake views and excellent New Zealand fare, plus an odd but tasty assortment of international dishes, makes **Echo Cliff**, 5 Tongariro St., tel. 88-539, popular with locals. Dinner on Friday through Sunday (with reservations) or smorgasbord lunch at the **Huka Homestead Restaurant**, tel. 82-245, in the historic village on Huka Falls Road combines exceptional sightseeing and dining. In town, **Brookes**, 22 Tuwharetoa Street, tel. 85-919, offers excellent value for the dollar with a range of menu items from seafood to steak dishes.

La Vielle France, 133 Tongariro Street, tel. 84-220, offers fine French provincial dishes and superb lake views.

Consider splurging at the **Huka Lodge**, 85-791, on the banks of the Waikato, where you'll fantasize about spending a week rather than merely having dinner. Conviviality, quiet elegance and exquisitely tasteful decor meld perfectly with pre-dinner and dinner drinks, food and wine selections, for less than

NZ$100 per person. In quite another sphere of splurging, the **THC Wairakei Hotel**'s main restaurant, tel. 48-021, is dress-up for an excellent dinner at about a quarter the Huka's price. You get what you pay for.

Itinerary Options from Rotorua

Mokoia Island in the middle of Lake Rotorua is reached by a two-hour launch cruise (Rotorua Launch Service, tel. 479-852) for a dip in Hinemoa's hot pool, NZ$18 adult, NZ$6 child. Lake Okataina, the most unspoiled of the lakes surrounding Rotorua, is reached by a scenic drive along lakes Rotoiti, Rotoehu and Rotomo. The Eastern Walkway (six-hour round trip) starts at the northern end of the lake at Tauranganui Bay and finishes four miles later at Humphries Bay on Lake Tarawera. Hell's Gate, ten miles east of Rotorua on Highway 30, consists of ten acres of volcanic activity highlighted by the Kakahi hot waterfall. Orakei Korako, 12 miles off the Rotorua-Taupo Highway, is one of the finest thermal areas. Board a jet boat to cross Lake Ohakuri, formed by a hydroelectric dam that submerged three-fourths of the silica deposits. The remaining terraces colored by sinter and algae are well worth seeing. Nearby is Alladins Cave with its mirror-like pool of jade green water. Flightseeing excursions (Floatplane Air Services, tel. 84-069) land on a strip on Mt. Tarawara's summit for a great view of the crater and surrounding region, NZ$60 per person.

Huka Village on Huka Falls Road, a little over a mile from Taupo, is an authentic reconstruction of a New Zealand pioneer village of a hundred years ago. Open daily 10:00 a.m. to 5:00 p.m., NZ$3.50 adult, children free.

If you have plenty of time, there are several intriguing possibilities for further explorations from Rotorua:

Lake Waikarenoana: Follow Highway 38 south of Rotorua to Wairoa on coastal Highway 2, then on to the unspoiled wilderness of Urewera National Park and the park's gem, Lake Waikaremoana. Driving is most convenient, but a bus from Rotorua to and through the park runs twice a week. On a summer afternoon, take the two-hour Huiarau launch trip around the lake from Home Bay. Visit the park and you'll find incredible vegetation and waterfalls—as well as fog, mist, and chronically wet conditions. The drive takes four to five hours and much of it is on unpaved road. The Wairoa bus goes there twice a week, on Tuesdays and Thursdays. Stop at park headquarters at Aniwaniwa for trail information, fishing permits, etc. In addition to many short walking trails, from November through March consider a five-day trek from Ruatahuna down the Whakatane Valley or three to four days on the Waikaremoana Track, starting at Onepoto, for vast panoramas and

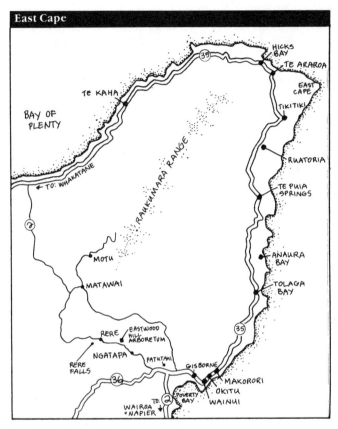

East Cape

beautiful views of the lake.

East Cape: Another alternative is to head eastward to Opitiki,
circling East Cape to Gisborne, 201 miles (2 days) of isolated
splendor, idyllic golden beaches and picnic spots with lots of
sunshine, camping on deserted sandy bays, ancient and
beautiful pohutukawa trees, rugged mountains creating major
rivers (Waiapu, Waipaoa and remote Motu) with outstanding
white water rafting and canoeing challenges, superb cycling,
and visits to elegantly carved Maori meeting houses. Along the
way there are two beautiful walkways: Anaura Bay Walkway
through the Anaura Scenic Reserve, and the Cooks Cove
Walkway at the end of Tolaga Bay, each less than six miles round
trip. When you finally arrive in Gisborne, the treat awaiting is
Bread and Roses restaurant (tel. 86-697) for excellent crepes,
quiches, vegetarian dishes and fresh bread.

DAY 9
LAKE TAUPO—TONGARIRO NATIONAL PARK—WANGANUI

Depart very early from Taupo for sightseeing on the slopes of Mt. Ruapehu in Tongariro National Park. From the Park, head for Wanganui, the "Garden City" on the Tasman Sea, for a relaxing evening.

Suggested Schedule	
8:00 a.m.	Breakfast and check out.
11:00 a.m.	Explore Taupo and have and early lunch.
1:00 p.m.	Leave Taupo for Turangi.
2:00 p.m.	Arrive in Turangi and visit the Trout Hatchery.
2:30 p.m.	Leave for Ohakune.
4:00 p.m.	Arrive in Ohakune and drive up Ohakune Mountain Rd. on Mt. Ruapehu. See the sunset from Turoa ski lift.
5:30 p.m.	Leave for Wanganui.
8:00 p.m.	Arrive in Wanganui, check in and prepare for dinner.
8:30 p.m.	Dinner and an evening stroll before bed.

Lake Taupo to Wanganui

Take Highway 1 to Turangi. Trout fishing is an option in the Tongariro River. Otherwise, visit the Tongariro Trout Hatchery, a little over a mile south of town on Highway 1. Look carefully for the small sign. From Turangi it is about an hour and a half drive to Ohakune on Highway 1, turning west on Highway 49 at Waiouru. This stretch of Highway 1 is called the Desert Road as it passes through Rangipo Desert, an inhospitable area of sand dunes and gravel created by the mountains that force prevailing westerlies to give up their moisture. From Ohakune you can drive straight up Mt. Ruapehu's southwestern flank on Ohakune Mountain Road. East of the Desert Road and the Parallel Tongariro River you drive past the Kaimanawa State Forest Park, entirely forested with mountain, red and silver beech. Return to Highway 49 west to Raetihi, where you'll turn south on Highway 4 to Wanganui, about a 2½ hour trip without any hurry.

Although travel is better by car, through lake and forest areas, desert and deep gorges, the main Auckland-Wellington railway line runs through the western part of the region, stopping at National Park, Ohakune and Taumarunui, where jetboats head

down the upper Wanganui River to Pipiriki. Jetboats and buses
continue down the Wanganui Valley to Wanganui. NZR Road
Services and Newmans buses serve all main points in the region
and south to Wellington and North to Auckland. Bonnici
Coachlines (tel. 58-456) also runs to Auckland and Wellington.
River City Tracks operates daily from Ohakune to Wanganui
(tel. 58-395).

Sightseeing Highlights

▲▲**Tongariro Trout Hatchery** tells about the history of trout
fishing in the area. In the underwater viewing chamber downstairs, you can observe trout of all sizes. In winter you can
watch the spawning process.

▲▲▲**Tongariro National Park**, New Zealand's first, consists
of three volcanoes: Tongariro (6,458 feet), Ngauruhoe (7,515
feet), and Ruapehu (9,175 feet). All three volcanoes have
erupted within memory, showering forest and scrub with hot
ash, most recently Mount Ruapehu in 1975. Rings of mud flows
surround the mountain below the snowline. Crater Lake at its
summit is warm and acidic, a shallow liquid lid for its smoldering volcanic depths. It is actually dangerous to descend the
steep cliffs surrounding Crater Lake, and conditions around the
lake vary with volcanic activity.

The Te Maari Crater on the north side of Tongariro, a truncated multiple volcano, shows signs of recent activity and lava
flows. The Te Maari Crater and the Red Crater on Tongariro, past
the Emerald Lakes, are steaming and sulphurous. The perfectly
symmetrical cone of Mount Ngauruhoe is the most active of the
three volcanos. For information and interesting displays covering the park's geology, volcanic activity, flora and fauna, hiking
trails and walking tours, stop at the Tongariro National Park
Headquarters in Whakapapa Village (tel. 729) or the Okakune
Ranger Station and Park Information Centre at the start of Okakune Road (tel. 58-578) from 8:00 a.m. to 5:00 p.m.

▲**Ohakune** is the start-off point for many rafting, fishing, hiking and canoeing trips, as well as the winter base for skiers in
the national park and the Kaimanawa State Forest Park. From
Ohakune drive up Ruapehu's southwestern flank traversing the
park's various climatic zones.

Where to Stay

For NZ$8 a night, you can stay at Wanganui's small (12 people)
YHA Hostel, 3 Tregenna St., tel. 42-804, at the mouth of the
Wanganui River near the beach and on a city bus line. The
YWCA, 232 Wicksteed St., tel. 57-480, is a comfortable small
house in the city center.

The cabins of the **Alwyn Motor Court**, 65 Karaka St., tel.

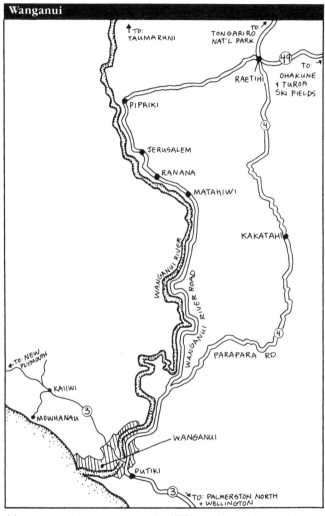

44-500, and those out at **Castlecliff Beach**, NZ$20 doubles, or at the beautifully situated **Aramoho Motor Camp**, Somme Parade, tel. 38-402, NZ$35 double, about four miles outside of town, have everything two people (or more) need. The old-fashioned and charming **Riverside Inn**, 2 Plymouth St., tel. 32-529, at NZ$33 double, is a small hotel close to the city center that is an equally good value.

The best quality hotels, serviced motels, motels and motor inns in Wanganui are NZ$46-$62 twin/double. Take your choice from more than a dozen with all facilities and amenities, in garden and park-like settings, within minutes of the city center: **Avro Motel**, 36 Alma Rd., tel. 55-279, with excellent caravan facilities; the **Acacia Park Motel**, 140 Anzac Parade, tel. 39-093, the **Collegiate Motor Inn**, 122 Liverpool St., tel. 59-309, the **River City Motel**, 30 Somme Parade, tel. 39-107, and others.

Where to Eat
For memorable meals in Wanganui, eat along the riverside or picnic in nearby parks. Plan to have lunch or dinner along the river at the inexpensive **Riverside Tavern Garden Bistro**, 33 Somme Parade, or the more pricey and less casual **Riverina Restaurant**, tel. 38-656.

Other alternatives are to pack a gourmet lunch at **The Cellers and Deli** for a trip to beautiful Virginia Park or wait until you get to the Park for lunch at the **Shangri-La Restaurant** on Great North Road.

In town, **Capers** in Victoria Court may be better looking, but one of the most pleasant eating experiences is a light lunch in the Tudor Court Arcade terrace at **Dr. Johnson's Coffee Lounge** on Victoria Avenue.

Itinerary Options
Lake Taupo—Turangi: Try the easy three-hour walk along the river from Taupo to Aratiatia or vice versa. Turangi, at the southern end of Lake Taupo on the banks of the Tongariro River, is the self-proclaimed "Heart of the Great New Zealand Outdoors" and "Trout Fishing Capital of the World." There you can be outfitted, licensed, and pumped full of valuable information to fish in the best places for brown trout in March-April and rainbow trout in May-September. Local fishing guides are available.

Rafting enthusiasts, contact **Turangi White Water Rafting** (tel. Turangi 8856) for whitewater thrills on the Tongariro or Mohaka Rivers or wilderness fishing trips. There is bus service to Turangi from all major and secondary cities.

Fly-fish on Lake Tarawera, where 9-10 lb. rainbow trout can be netted during the May-June spawning season.

Tongariro National Park: For "trampers," the Ketetahi Track from Highway 47 near Lake Rotaira to the Mangatepopo trail hut offers great views over hundreds of square miles to the north, including all of Lake Taupo. As an alternative to this two to three day hike, Venture Treks, a local guide service, offers a five-day guided trek, the Mount Ruapehu Alpine Walk, around the mountain to Ruapehu's crater lake. In summer, a walk from Whakapapa Village to the summit of Mt. Tongariro offers breathtaking views across Tongariro National Park to Lake Taupo, the Kaimanawas and Mt. Egmont. In winter, Whakapapa is an enormous skifield, mostly for intermediate and advanced skiers, with an uphill capacity of 13,500 skiers an hour. Combine excellent spring skiing with incredible trout fishing or local white-water rafting in the Tongariro or Rangitikei Rivers. National Park Headquarters in Whakapapa will supply all needed information, maps, hunting licenses and suggested guide services. Just 11 miles from Ohakune and an hour's drive from Whakapapa on the southern slopes of Mt. Ruapehu, the Turoa skifield offers plenty of slopes for all levels of skiers.

If you decide to stay over in the Tongariro National Park, here are the range of choices: Ohakune's **YHA Hostel** (tel. 58-724) is next to the Turoa Information Centre. The **Whakapapa Motor Camp** (tel. Ruapehu 897) has the largest variety of accommodations: tent sites, caravan sites, nice cabins (only NZ$24 for a four-berth), and a lodge with bunks.

Rates for hotels, better self-contained ski chalets and lodges with private facilities have zoomed upwards in the last few years but still offer good values when compared to accommodations in U.S. ski areas. Rates are about 30% lower in summer. The **Ruapehu Skotel** (tel. Ruapehu 619) is NZ$90-$100 double in ski season. Consider spending a night at the elegant and internationally renowned **THC Chateau Tongariro** (tel. Ruapehu 809) as one of your legitimate budget breakers for the trip (NZ$125). The Chateau is right in the center of all skiing and touring activities in an area where accommodations are very limited.

Turangi is an ideal touring base for both National Park and Taupo-Tongariro area activities, with a wide variety of accommodations, camping and caravan parks. Campers should consider heading for the **Mahuia Campground** about three miles from National Park on Highway 47, one of the best in New Zealand—and free.

The Wanganui River Road is an alternative to heading south on Highway 4 from Raetihi to Wanganui. Adjacent to the river are good trails to waterfalls, the remains of Maori villages, scenic lookouts in the hills above the river, and Jerusalem, one of the most photogenic villages on the North Island, nestling on a green carpet in a bush-rimmed riverbend, red roofs on white walls surrounding a delicate church spire. Above Pipiriki, to Taumaruni, the river and its 239 rapids are navigable only by jetboats or canoes. Contact **Pipiriki Jet Boat Tours** (tel. Raetihi 54633) for information.

DAY 10
WANGANUI-WELLINGTON

Take a relaxing break from driving. Stroll in Wanganui's lovely parks, travel by riverboat up the tranquil Wanganui for a wine-tasting tour, and visit a regional museum before driving down the scenic west ("Kapiti") coast to Wellington on very good roads.

Suggested Schedule

8:30 a.m.	Breakfast.
9:30 a.m.	Drurie Hill vistas.
10:30 a.m.	Visit your choice of parks or museum.
12:30 p.m.	Lunch and check out.
2:00 p.m.	Tour the Holly Lodge Estate Winery along the Wanganui River.
4:30 p.m.	Return to Wanganui and depart for Wellington.
6:30 p.m.	Break for dinner near Levin on the west coast.
9:00 p.m.	Arrive in Wellington and check in.

Transportation
Highway 1 to Wellington, the most direct route down the Kapiti Coast, has pretty pastoral scenes followed by good beach stops and outstanding sea views. The region around Levin is a major fruit and vegetable producing area. In season, pick up your lunch at roadside stands. Starting at Levin, Highway 1 runs between the coast and the Tararua Range, with forest-covered 2000- to 3000-foot mountains.

Heading south from Levin is a long stretch of golden sand beaches—Waikanae, Paraparaumu and Raumati—in Wellington's suburbs. Avid shell collectors, bring large bags to Paekakariki. South of Paekakariki take the winding Paekakariki Hill Road for good views of Porirua Harbor to the southwest.

Sightseeing Highlights
▲▲**Wanganui**'s tree-lined riverfront, green hills and many lovely parks make it one of New Zealand's more picturesque cities. Visit the "Garden City's" Cook's Gardens, Queen's Park, the Aramoho Park, Moutoa Gardens, Victoria Park, Peat Park, and especially beautiful Virgina Lake. Also see Bushy Park, 15 miles northwest of Wanganui, a fine old home with spacious gardens and a bush park, open Wednesday to Sunday, 10:00 a.m. to 5:00 p.m. Drop in the Hospitality Wanganui Information

Centre on Guyton St. for maps, brochures and even a person-alized tour guide (free).

▲▲**The Wanganui River** offers a pleasant riverboat (or jet-boat) ride up the lower river. For information on the historic *MV Waireka* riverboat trip to Hipango Park with a stop at the Holly Lodge Estate, tel. 36-346. NZ$17 adult, NZ$8.50 child. For jet boat info, contact Wanganui River Jet Tours, tel. 36-346.

▲▲**Wanaganui Regional Museum** in Queen's Park, one of the best in the country, houses a large and exceptional Maori collection, including a 75-foot war canoe. Open weekdays from 9:30 a.m. to 4:30 p.m., weekends 1:00 to 4:30 p.m.

▲▲**Durie Hill** (216 feet) at the south end of the Wanganui Bridge provides a splendid view of the region. Take the elevator to a platform at the summit. For an even better view, if you're energetic, ascend the Durie Hill War Memorial Tower.

Where to Stay
The Ivanhoe Inn, 52 Ellice St., tel. 842-264, on the Mount Victoria hillside, has spacious singles, twins and double rooms to offer hostelers at NZ$10-$24. Also on Mount Victoria, **Beethoven House**, 89 Brougham St., tel. 842-226, is a non-YHA "B&B-hostel" for non-smokers who love (or can tolerate) continuous Beethoven, and can afford NZ$11. In the center of town, convenient to all transportation and attractions, the **YHA Hostel**, 40 Tinakori Rd., tel. 736-271, is NZ$11. Campers should plan to find sites outside of Wellington such as the **Hutt Park Motor Camp**, 95 Hutt Park Rd., tel. 685-913, at NZ$6 for two. As an alternative, try the **YHA Hostel**, no phone, in the hill country of Kaitoke at the top of the Hutt Valley.

There is no YMCA or YWCA, but the 170-room **Railton Travel Hotel**, 213 Cuba St., tel. 851-632, a B&B with the op-tion of three meals, is the next best thing. The double rate of NZ$45 is a bargain. The 60-unit **Rowena Budget Travel Hotel**, 115 Brougham St., tel. 857-872, is a comparably good B&B value. For hilltop views of the city and harbor, plenty of exercise for those without cars, thick with character and comfort, try the **Fairview Lodge**, 8 Church St., tel. 726-248, a B&B at NZ$40 double.

Look for inexpensive lodging (NZ$48 for a twin/double) out-side of Wellington, such as the **Spinnaker Motel**, tel. 33-8171, in Plimmerton or the **Safari Park Motel**, tel. 36-054, in Wai-kanae. In a year, in-town "budget" motel flat rates have gone up from NZ$54 to NZ$65 for central, fully equipped and attractive units, such as those of **The Apollo Lodge**, 49 Majoribanks St., tel. 851-849, the **Majoribanks Apartments**, 38 Majoribanks St., tel. 857-305, and the **Wellington Luxury Motel**, 14 Hob-son St., tel. 726-825.

Among downtown hotels with superior or luxury standards, which means over NZ$110 for a twin/double, the very attractive and central **West Plaza**, 110 Wakefield St., tel. 731-440, stands out for two or three persons at NZ$90. An extravagent splurge on the Terrace above the business district, the **James Cook Hotel** on The Terrace, tel. 725-865, at NZ$125-$150 single, twin or double, literally stands above the rest. As a bonus, lifts descend to the city as well as up to the rooms.

Where to Eat
For the best combination of views of harbor and city, food, service and atmosphere, take the Kelburn cable car to the **Skyline**, 1 Upland Road, Kelburn, tel. 758-727. Or, if the cable car ride, fresh air and twinkling stars go to your head, you can try to get a table at **Marbles**, Kelburn Villas, tel. 758-490, or **Le Routier** (92 Upland Road, tel. 758-981.

Otherwise, you'll find good-to-excellent restaurants and cafes all over Wellington. For a plentiful salad bar, try **Suzie's Coffee Bar and Restaurant** at 108 Willis St., or soup and salads at **The Great New Zealand Soup Kitchen**, 32 Waring Taylor St. near Lambton Quay. For natural foods, an excellent choice is **That's Natural**, 88 Manners Street, tel. 736-681; or **Amrita Vegetarian Restaurant**, 127 Cuba Mall.

Before leaving the North Island, try the great charcoaled steaks at **Beefeater**, 105 The Terrace, tel. 738-195. **Il Casino**, 108 Tory St., tel. 857-496, is the best North Italian restaurant in New Zealand for decor and fine pasta, seafood, gnocchi and other tasty dishes. The French restaurant with the best views of the harbor is **Grain of Salt**, 232 Oriental Parade, tel. 848-642. If you prefer just darn good hamburgers and sundaes, stop down the street at **Rockefellers**, 132 Oriental Parade, tel. 846-975.

Around Country Place, restaurants seem to progress alphabetically up the street: rarified atmosphere and prices at the **Bacchus**, 8 Courtney Place, tel. 846-592, where you can order anything confidently; BYO French lunch or dinner at **Chez Nigel** 29A Courtney Place, tel. 844-535; **Java**, 99 Courtney Place, tel. 857-620, for one of the most interesting dining experiences in Wellington; and delicious venison dishes at **Marcel's**, 104 Courtney Place, tel. 842-159.

Itinerary Options
Consider a wine trip via paddlewheeler (tel. 39-344) to the Holly Lodge Estate Winery. The *Otonui* has been on the river for 80 years. The 2½-hour trip departs Monday through Friday at 10:00 a.m., weekends 10:00 a.m. and 2:00 p.m., NZ$11 adult, NZ$5 child. From the winery, take the jetboat ride to Hipango

Park. Holly Lodge operates these jetboat tours, which leave at 10:00 a.m. and 2:00 p.m. for the 12-mile trip to Hipango Park Scenic Reserve (two hours round-trip).

For a special adventure, try a jetboat ride up the most scenic and exciting stretch of the Wanganui River north of Pipiriki. Choose the most interesting places on the river from a local map (see the PRO) and select the corresponding jetboat tour, from 35-minute local tours to trips to Hipango Park (12 miles), Manapurua, Drap Scene, costing about NZ$22-$50 for adults.

John Hammond's River Road Tours offers a complete river tour by minibus with a stop in the picturesque Maori village of Jerusalem.

DAY 11
WELLINGTON

Enjoy leisurely sightseeing on Marine Drive, overlooking the
harbor from many different viewpoints, followed by a cable car
ride for dinner and views of the city from the Kelburn Terminal
area. In between, tour the City's most interesting architectural,
historical and cultural attractions. All the while, enjoy no fog,
no smog, and no pollution in "Windy Wellington."

Suggested Schedule

8:30 a.m.	Breakfast.
9:30 a.m.	Depart for Marine Drive.
12:00 noon	Picnic lunch along Marine Drive.
1:30 p.m.	Drop off your car, then tour Parliament buildings.
2:30 p.m.	National Museum and Art Gallery.
4:00 p.m.	Cable car to Kelburn and the Botanic Gardens.
6:00 p.m.	Dinner and evening at the Top of Victoria.

Transportation
The Wellington City Corporation bus system mainly operates
south of the city. Trains are used to the north. Eastern, western
and southern bus routes start at the railroad station on Waterloo
Quay or at Courtenay Place. Pick up timetables from newstands.
Four commuter trains run to Upper and Lower Hutt and other
northern destinations. NZRR buses run up the peninsula's west
coast and center (tel. 725-399 for bus and rail information.)
Newmans Coach Tours operate east coast intercity services.
Mount Cook Landlines runs between Wellington and Auckland
(11 hours). Day (Silver Fern) and night (Northerner) trains to
Auckland and intermediate points leave Monday to Saturday
from the New Zealand Railways Terminal.

Orientation
Approach Wellington along the "Gold Coast," actually an
elongated suburb on the western edge of the southern Peninsula. The rugged mountain forests of the Rimutakas and Tararua
Ranges separate the Wairapa Plain to the east from the western
coastal area.
    New Zealand's capital city at the tip of this peninsula is set in
a green amphitheater on a sparkling harbor. On a sunny and
windy day, Wellington becomes a very beautiful city. Wellington can be best appreciated from the Cook Straits ferry heading

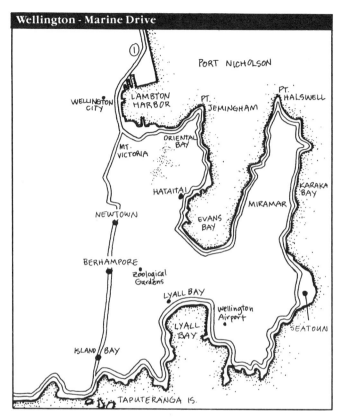

Wellington - Marine Drive

through the harbor, from atop Mount Victoria or at various points on the 24-mile Marine Drive, especially from the north side of Miramar Peninsula. The winds funnelling through Wellington from Cook Strait produce crisp, clear views of the surrounding forested peninsulas, the pastel wooden buildings climbing the hills above Oriental Bay, and the conglomeration of government and office buildings rimming the waterfront.

On weekends the government and corporate population disappears and, unlike Auckland, it's a good time to visit and bargain for reduced hotel rates. Otherwise book in advance. Good city bus service from the railway station will take care of your transportation needs. For bookings and other information, use the Information Office at the railway center or the Government Tourist Bureau.

Sightseeing Highlights
▲▲**Marine Drive** hugs the harbor shore for 24 miles, skirting

Oriental and Evans Bay, looping around Miramar Peninsula, where there are fine views of the harbor at the Massey Memorial. Several soft sandy swimming beaches, including Scorching, Karaka and Worser Bays in the inner harbor and Lyall and Island Bays in the outer harbor, offer inviting places to stop and see spectacular bush-covered hills around the bright blue bay waters.

▲The circular domed **Parliament**, the "Beehive," houses the government's executive offices. Free tours are conducted hourly from 9:00 a.m. to 3:30 p.m.

▲**The Old Government Building** at the northern end of Lambton Quay is one of the largest all-wooden buildings in the world. In a city where old edifices are rapidly being replaced by modern office structures, this wooden Italianate civic building is all the more rare and precious.

▲▲**The National Museum** has an excellent Maori and Pacific Island collection (11:00 a.m. to 4:45 p.m. daily). Also see the adjoining National Art Gallery, with New Zealand and international art.

▲**City Council's 2½-hour afternoon bus tour**, costing NZ$8, is an inexpensive and easy way to see all of Wellington's sightseeing highlights.

▲▲▲**Cable cars** climb for about four minutes up to the Kelburn terminal from Cable Car Lane off Lambton Quay in the heart of the shopping district. The cost is NZ$.55 adult, NZ$.25 child, one-way. From there, walk down through the Botanic Gardens and the Lady Norwood Rose Gardens, through Thorndon, where some of the city's older wooden cottages (dating from the 1870s) cluster on Ascot Street.

DAY 12
WELLINGTON TO CHRISTCHURCH

Over a thousand years ago the original Polynesian settlers in the
Marlborough Sounds region started hunting moa, the giant
flightless relative of the ostrich, until inevitable extinction. Four
hundred Maoris watched in astonishment as Capt. James Cook's
HMS Endeavor sailed past in 1770. Abel Tasman had been the
first European arrival, 128 years before the *Endeavor* dropped
anchor, but Tasman stayed only a few days before sailing north.
After claiming the land for the King and naming the sound for
Queen Charlotte, Cook circumnavigated the South Island,
returned to the Sound for reprovision, and sailed back to
England, revisiting the Sound four more times for a total of 15
weeks between 1770 and 1777. The bush-covered hillsides of
Queen Charlotte Sound that you pass aboard the Inter-Island
Ferry from Wellington to Picton were heavily forested in Cook's
time. Today you'll still have no difficulty understanding why it
was one of his favorite anchorages.

As in the Bay of Islands, closer to the equator but actually less
sunny and warm, you can charter yachts and cruisers, rent
fishing boats of all kinds and find a remote island, bay or cove
with white sand beaches for a get-away day or week, or join a
variety of cruises almost any time of day. There's over 600 miles
of coastline to choose from. Behind the Sounds are warm hills
and valleys with fruit orchards and vineyards, national parks
with trout filled lakes and rivers, and even mountains for skiing.

Suggested Schedule

7:00 a.m.	Breakfast and check out.
9:00 a.m.	Inter-Island Ferry across Cook Strait to Picton. Lunch on board.
2:00 p.m.	Train or bus to Christchurch.
8:00 p.m.	Arrive Christchurch and check in.
9:00 p.m.	Late dinner and evening stroll along the Avon.

Transportation
I recommend that you turn in your rented car in Wellington
(without penalty or one-way charge) and pick up another car in
Christchurch from the same rental company, continuing your
weekly rental agreement.

Between Wellington and Picton on the South Island there are
four ferry services daily each way. For NZ$16.70 (cars from
NZ$70 depending on size), the crossing in daylight and with

good weather is a scenic, fun trip.

The train, which is more quaint than comfortable, leaves the Picton station near the ferry landing at 2:10 p.m. and arrives in Christchurch at 8:05 p.m. The cost, NZ$20.60, is a little more than Newman's bus service, which also meets the ferry and gets to Christchurch a bit faster. Take your choice: more comfort on the bus, a more unusual travel experience on the train.

If you decide to drive, book ferry space for the car or camper van as far in advance as possible (months ahead, for travel during Australian holidays). The wharf terminal buildings at Wellington are off Aotea Quay. The turnoff is clearly marked by road signs. Report one hour before sailing time. Driver and passengers must have passenger tickets.

From Picton, train and bus travelers as well as drivers will follow Highway 1 south through Blenheim, along the Seaward Kaikaura range and its narrow, wild indented coastline. In Kaikaura, motorists can take a break in the six-hour trip to walk along the shoreline and have refreshments.

Sightseeing Highlight
▲▲▲**Marlborough Sounds Maritime Park** region contains a marvelous variety of outdoor recreation. From Picton, Havelock and Motueka, rent charter yachts, line-fishing boats, and game-fishing boats, cruise to sandy bays, coves, islands and their virtually untouched beaches in the region's deep inlets. The rangers' offices in Blenheim and Havelock, as well as local Visitors' Information offices, have all the necessary maps, guides and other information.

Where to Stay
Christchurch has an abundance of good and reasonably priced accommodations on public transportation lines.

There are two hostels in Christchurch: the **Cora Wilding Youth Hostel**, 9 Evelyn Couzins Ave., tel. 899-199, in a charming old mansion 15 minutes walk from Cathedral Square; and **Rolleston House**, 5 Worcester St., tel. 66-564, ten minutes closer to the center. Both charge NZ$10.

Within three to six miles from the Square, first-rate caravan sites are available for NZ$11 for two persons, some with cabins or tourist flats from NZ$25 to NZ$36: **Amber Park**, 308 Blenheim Rd., tel. 483-327; **Meadow Park Motor Camp**, 39 Meadow St., tel. 529-176; and **Russley Park Motor Camp**, 372 Yaldhurst Rd., tel. 427-021.

Many excellent guest houses charge NZ$45-$50 double or NZ$25 single, and there are a few real B&B bargains. Just one block from the square, comfort, simplicity and reasonable price (NZ$23-$28 double or twin) make the **Hereford Private**

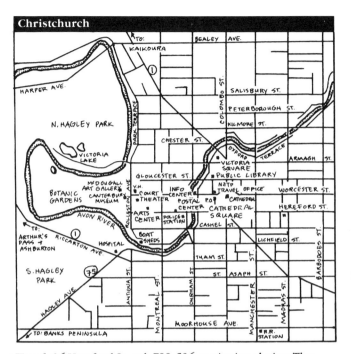

Christchurch

Hotel, 36 Hereford St., tel. 799-536, a winning choice. The love and attention lavished on the interior furnishing and decorations of the **Eliza's Manor House**, 82 Bealey Ave., tel, 68-584, a historic trust mansion, makes this B&B a bargain at NZ$25 per person. The cozy **Aaragi Guest House**, 15 Riccarton Rd., tel. 483-584, NZ$42 double and twin, is further out but has public transit at the door. With 37 nicely decorated rooms at NZ$25 per person, the very popular **Windsor Private Hotel B&B**, 52 Armagh St., tel. 61-503, offers better odds than the other guest houses for room availability. The **Warners Hotel**, tel. 65-159, an old B&B landmark on the Square, charges NZ$23 per person. From guest kitchen, to rooms and garden, everything is comfortable about the **Wolseley Lodge**, 107 Papanui Rd., tel. 556-202 including the price: NZ$23 per person. The **Hotel Melville**, 49 Gloucester St., tel. 798-956, at NZ$19 also is worth checking out.

There are countless very good motels in Christchurch at NZ$45 and up. NZ$55 for two persons gets you a choice of five-star motels. "Bargains" in good motels, both close-in and further out, cost NZ$31-$39: the **City Court**, 850 Colombo St., tel. 69-099; **Fairlane Court Motel**, 69 Linwood Ave., tel.

894-943; **Holiday Lodge Motel**, 862 Colombo St., tel. 66-584; and **Salisbury Motel**, 206 Salisbury St., tel. 68-713.

Where to Eat
An ample variety of cafes and tearooms are distributed around Christchurch to take care of breakfast and lunch needs, but a visit to the Garden City merits something a bit more special. Smorgasbord fans shouldn't pass up **The Gardens Restaurant and Tea Kiosk**, tel. 65-076, in the Botanic Gardens. French provincial fare at the **Restaurante Sorbonne**, tel. 50-566, or a bowl of soup and veggies at the **Dux de Lux Gormet Vegetarian Restaurant**, tel. 66-919, both sharing the atmosphere of the Christchurch Arts Centre on Montreal St., make excellent lunch choices. Also, enjoy smoked salmon at **Grimsby's**, Montreal St., tel. 799-040, wonderful old building, or a fish and salad lunch, with delicious desserts, at the **Greenhouse Restaurant**, 663A Colombo St., tel. 68-524.

You won't be overwhelmed by the outstanding dinner choices in Christchurch. Two places that easily could qualify are the **Sign of the Takahe**, tel. 324-052, in a wonderful stone building with great views of the Lyttelton Harbour Estuary and Christchurch from the Cashmere Hills, excellent international cuisine and service, and the waterfront location and excellent French-style food at BYO **Scarborough Fare** in Sumner, seven miles southeast of Christchurch, tel. 27-6987.

Other recommended dining alternatives include: **Leinster**, 158 Leinster Road, Merivale, tel. 588-866; **Michael's**, 178 High Street, tel. 60-822; steak at the **Forget-Me-Not**, 12 Wakefield Street, Sumner, tel. 26-6501, about seven miles southeast of Christchurch; and the *prix fixe* French menu at **Portstone**, 471 Ferry Road, tel. 896-529. Extra large appetites will be well rewarded by a visit to the **Wagon Wheel Restaurant**, Papanui Rd., tel. 556-159, for steak, chicken, seafood and excellent deserts. Craving salad along with the same basics, try the **Jail Restaurant**, 106 Gloucester St., tel. 66-553.

Itinerary Options
If you have plenty of time, instead of heading directly to Christchurch, tour in the Marlborough Sounds Region. Visit Nelson's Botanic Gardens, Matai Valley and Tahuna Beach. Thirty-five miles to the northwest is Kaiteriteri, the best beach in the area. (Watch out for the katipo, a poisonous spider that lurks in beach driftwood.) See the view of Tasman Bay from Takaka Hill. The Nelson area's high quality pottery clays have contributed to a thriving pottery craft in Nelson, Hope, Brightwater and Wakefield. Lots of ceramics, glasswork, weav-

ing, jewelry, woodcraft, and other arts and crafts are also found in the Nelson area.

Sail in beautiful Kenepuru Sound off Pelorus Sound. Pelorus is the most extensive sound (32 miles) with the finest scenery. Fish for cod, terakiki, snapper, garfish, grouper and kahawai. Surfcast between Kaikoura and Cape Koamaru. Flyfish in the Rai, Pelorus, Wairau and Opawa Rivers and Spring Creek for brown trout. In summer, try salmon fishing in the Wairau River.

Visit vineyards in Redwoods Valley, Ruby Bay, Upper Moutere and especially Blenheim's Wairau Valley. Ski in Rainbow Valley, west of Blenheim and enjoy outstanding views. Flightsee over the region from Nelson, Blenheim and Motueka.

From Nelson head west on Highway 60 toward Motueka and Abel Tasman National Park with its golden beaches, rocky headlands and tidal inlets. Enter the Park at Marohau. To return, hire a taxi from Motueka to pick you up in Totaranui, at the north end of the park, or charter a boat in Motueka or Kaiteriteri. A simpler alternative might be Abel Tasman National Park Enterprises' four-day launch trip and guided walk, which includes three nights at The Lodge at Torrent Bay.

In the North-West Nelson State Forest (930,000 acres) is one of New Zealand's best known tracks, the Heaphy Track, a 42-mile (one-way), five-day hike linking Golden Bay at the Abel Tasman National Park with the west coast. There are seven huts and five shelters, but they can be crowded any time of year so pack your own tent.

DAY 13
CHRISTCHURCH REGION

Stroll along the Avon, people-watch in Cathedral Square, visit the museums and Arts Centre, see Gothic and Victorian architecture, and experience the tranquility of Christchurch. Leave Christchurch in the afternoon over the Port Hills to Lyttelton, then return to the urbane delights of the city's center.

Suggested Schedule

8:00 a.m.	Leisurely breakfast.
9:00 a.m.	Stroll along the Avon and walking tour around city center.
12:00 noon	Picnic lunch on the banks of the Avon.
1:00 p.m.	Port Hills drive.
6:30 p.m.	Dinner.
8:30 p.m.	Attend theater at the Arts Center.

Orientation

Christchurch was planned by a young English Tory, John Robert Godley, to be an English city, and the magnificent parks and gardens adjoining the serpentine Avon River attest to that vision. In contrast to other New Zealand cities, the city's center is a pleasure for pedestrians. It is a city to be seen on bicycle, foot and boat.

Colonial wooden architecture has fine examples such as the homes along Bealey Avenue and the McLeans Mansion on Manchester Street; distinguished commercial buildings including the Pegasus Press building in Oxford Terrace and the Occidental Hotel in Hereford.

The city's urban amenities balance its regional outdoor recreation and scenic highlights: the inner city with the beautiful Avon, Hagley Park and Botanic Gardens, and Cathedral Square, and the city's perimeter with Summit Road atop Port Hills, the very special Banks Peninsula, and picturesque Canterbury farms. Further afield are Rakaia, Rangitata, and Waimakariri Rivers and lakes for fishing or rafting, snow-clad Mt. Hutt, thermal Hamner Springs' hills and exotic forests and the spectacular Arthur's Pass National Park. The Canterbury Information Centre (75 Worcester St., at the corner of Oxford Terrace, tel. 799-629) and the NZTP Travel Office (Government Life Building, Cathedral Square, tel. 794-900) will take care of most of your needs for information, maps, brochures, bookings, tickets

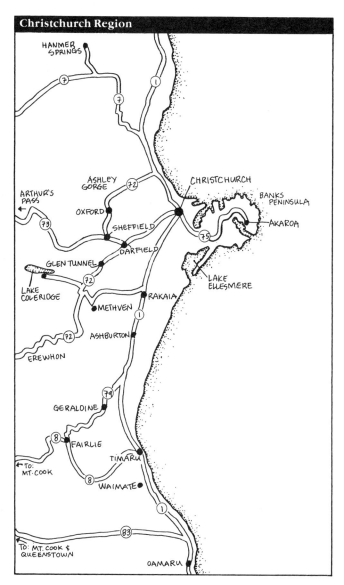

Christchurch Region

for local attractions, vehicle rentals and tours. For complete information and advice on outdoor activities and tour operators in the Christchurch region, visit the Outdoor Recreation Centre in the Arts Centre (tel. 799-395).

Inner Canterbury Walking Tour
Cathedral Square is the center of the city. Colombo Street
runs north and south through it. From the entrance to the cathedral, Worcester Street leads west toward Hagley Park. Christchurch Cathedral (Anglican), the finest Gothic style church in
New Zealand, soars almost 200 feet. Climb the 133 narrow
stone steps through the bell chamber to the balconies of the
tower 100 feet above the Square where you get a great view of
the city, plains and even the Southern Alps on a clear day.

From the Square, walk one block north on Columbo Street to
Victoria Square, turn through the Square to Victoria Street and
the **Avon River**. Gracefully winding its way through the city,
the grassy banks dotted with flowerbeds, weeping willows and
old oaks, daffodils in spring and ornate bridges is the main
feature of Christchurch's "English" character and charm. Bicycles and canoes are the best ways to tour the Avon and the
historic and modern buildings lining the river.

Cross the Avon to the **floral clock artwork** in Victoria
Street at the corner of Chestnut on the way to the **Town Hall**
on Kilmore Street. In a city of history and fine old buildings,
this very modern glass-and-marble structure is a bold contrast.
You can stroll through the building weekdays between 9:00
a.m. and 5:00 p.m. or take a guided tour between 11:00 a.m.
and 3:00 p.m. for NZ$1.50 adult, NZ$.75 child. Outside is the
beautiful **Ferrier Fountain**. Continue along the Avon to the
Gothic **Provincial Government Buildings** on the corner of
Durham and Armagh Streets, built between 1859 and 1865, the
only remaining provincial government buildings in New Zealand
(the system was abolished in 1876). The Stone Chamber is open
daily from 9:00 a.m. to 4:00 p.m.

At Worcester Street turn left (west) to the **Arts Centre of
Christchurch**. Housed in the neo-gothic former University of
Canterbury, the Centre is now the home for day and evening
performing and visual arts, craft, dramatic, instrumental and
choral groups, shopping and restaurants. If you're strolling on
Saturday during the summer, an Arts, Crafts and Antique Market
is held in the Centre from 10:00 a.m. to 3:00 p.m. The Arts Centre Information Office in the clock tower is open for information
and bookings daily from 8:30 a.m. to 5:00 p.m. (tel. 60-988).

Across Rolleston Avenue, at the entrance to the Botanic
Gardens and adjacent to the **McDougall Art Gallery**, the
region's major art museum, is the **Canterbury Museum**. The
museum contains outstanding displays of early Maori culture
during the moa hunting era, mounted birds, Oriental art, a
reconstruction of colonial Christchurch, and the Hall of Antarctic Discovery. Open daily from 10:00 a.m. to 4:30 p.m. Behind
the museum, bounded by a loop of the Avon, is the **Botanic**

Gardens, full of native New Zealand plants, tropical, flowering, alpine and desert plants, orchids, flowering trees and much more. You may decide to return after lunch and spend more time in both the Museum and the gardens.

Sightseeing Highlights
▲▲▲The Avon River and its grassy tree-shaded banks winding around Christchurch's inner city provides a superb pathway, on foot, bicycle or water, to visit the primary attractions between Hadley Park/Botanic Gardens and Victoria Square/Town Hall. Rent a canoe from Antigua Boatsheds and follow the tree-lined Avon downstream past riverside parks, the Chamber of Commerce Building, Victoria Bridge, the Christchurch Town Hall and nearby floral clock in Victoria Square, passing under many picturesque bridges, notably the Bridge of Remembrance. Enjoy a two-hour riverside walk if you have the time.

▲▲Cathedral Square is surrounded by gift and souvenir shops. North of the square, New Regent Street, Columbo Street and a network of arcades are full of boutiques and specialty and antique shops. See the Christchurch Cathedral tower's panoramic view of the city (9:00 a.m. to 4:00 p.m. weekdays and Saturday, 12:30 to 4:30 p.m. on Sunday). Red buses from Cathedral Square leave at 1:30 p.m. for a city and suburb tour.

▲▲Town Hall is New Zealand's most striking modern town hall design.

▲Ferrier Fountain outside the Christchurch Town Hall and the **Bowler Fountain** in Victoria Square both light up at night with varied patterns of water and color.

▲▲The Art Centre Museum and Art Gallery, formerly the University, is a focal point for local artists, musicians, craftspeople, and all types of performers, on stage and in many shops, with an open air market on Saturdays in the summer. Check the current calendar for theater, ballet and other dance, recitals and arts and crafts exhibits.

▲▲The Nga-Hua-E-Wha National Marae, comprised of a meeting house, arts and crafts center, and the Riki-Rangi Carving Centre in the Arts Centre, is a showcase of local and New Zealand Maori culture.

▲▲The Canterbury Museum, directly across from the Arts Centre, has the finest Antarctic collection in the world as well as fine colonial and Maori sections. Open 10:00 a.m. to 4:30 p.m. weekdays, 2:00 to 4:30 p.m. Sunday.

▲▲The Botanic Gardens—75 acres include spectacular displays of exotic and native plants and trees. Open 8:00 a.m. to dusk.

▲The City Mall Complex contains the Shades Shopping Precinct, Cashfields and the National Mutual Arcade. It is linked by an overhead pedestrian walkway to the Canterbury Centre and the Triangle Centre.

Fine old gothic-style buildings, dating from the 1870s, dot the city center: the Canterbury Provincial Government Buildings, the Arts Centre, Canterbury Museum, and the State Trinity Centre; and neo-Gothic or High Victorian church design in wood and stone: Cathedral Church of Christ, St. Michael's, All Angels Church, and Cathedral of the Blessed Sacrament.

▲▲**Hadley Park**, a 450-acre haven close to the city center, in spring has thousands of daffodils blooming in Daffodil Woodland, and azaleas and rhododendrons in Milbrook Reserve off North Hagley Park.

▲**Port Hills** on Christchurch's outskirts has walkways with spectacular vistas: Sign of the Takahe, Crater Rim, Mount Vernon, Sign of the Kiwi, Victoria Park, Nicholson Park, Scarborough, Godley Head, the Bridle Path, Rapaki Track, Kennedy's Bush Track, Major Hornbrook's Track and the Bowenvale Walkway. To reach these walkways, head for Summit Road atop the Port Hills, an outstanding drive or bus tour to Lyttelton Harbour. From heights of over 1800 feet, the Northern Summit Road has views of Christchurch, the Seaward Kaikouras to the north, the Southern Alps, and the Canterbury Plains, and views of many reserves, lookouts and walkways.

▲**Ferrymead Historic Park**, a 100-acre site next to the Heathcote River, includes train and tram rides through vintage township and museum areas displaying the history of aeronautics, music instruments, printing, motor- and horse-drawn vehicles, fire-fighting, military and photographic equipment, urban transport and railways. Open 10:00 a.m. to 4:30 p.m. daily.

Christchurch has a wealth of other transport museums: the **Yaldhurst Transport Museum** with horse-drawn vehicles, vintage cars, racing cars, steam engines and traction engines; the **Steam Museum** at McLeans Island; and the **Royal New Zealand Air Force Museum**, with 18 aircraft dating from 1910 to the 1970s.

Itinerary Options

The Northern and Southern Summit Roads, both of which circle Governor's Bay, return to the city over Gebbie's Pass. Each route is about 60 miles long or 120 miles round-trip. For the Northern Summit Road, from Hereford Street adjoining Cathedral Square take High Street southeast, which becomes Ferry Road when it crosses Highway 1 (Madras Street). Head toward Lyttelton through Sumner, turning south (right) onto Summit Road. For the Southern Summit Road take Columbo but turn right on Summit Road. At Gebbies Pass Road turn right to Highway 75. To the right, Highway 75 leads back to the city; to the left, out to Banks Peninsula and Akaroa (see Day 22). The Christchurch Transport Board (tel. 794-600) has a three-hour Port Hills and Harbor Tour with a Lyttelton Harbor launch cruise (NZ$12 adult, NZ$8 child). NZRR Services offers a day-long trip covering both Northern and Southern Summit Roads for NZ$17 per person (tel. 799-020). Try walking the Bridle Path to Lyttelton Harbor (2 hours), or the Godley Head Walkway across Summit Road (2 hours).

Lyttelton, the South Islands leading port, located on the flanks of a flooded volcanic crater, has a fine collection of 19th century buildings and churches. Regular launches shuttle to the attractive Diamond Harbor on the south side of the harbor (tel. Lyttelton 28-8368).

Waimakariri River Gorges, 85 miles round-trip from Christchurch, is famed for trout and salmon fishing. From the Main West Road through Darfield and Sheffield, cross the Waimakariri River to the Gorge. Try a Waimakariri or Rakaia jet-boat or a raft tour for a half-day, day or two days. Rafting tours also operate on the Waiau, Hurunui and Rangitata Rivers. (North of Oxford, follow the turn-off to the Ashley River Gorge, returning to Christchurch via Rangiora and Belfast.)

Salmon fishing in the Rakaia, Rangitata and Waimakariri Rivers is from October 1 to April 30, with the best runs in December-March. October-December are noted for sea-run trout in all local rivers, and brown trout throughout the season. Rainbow and brown trout, landlocked salmon, and brook trout are found in Lakes Taylor, Sumner, Coleridge, Lyndon and Selfe from early November to the end of April. Excellent sea fishing is available around river mouths. Kawhai (Australian salmon) and cod are the main species caught. For the best locations for river, lake and seas fishing, use the services of one of the many excellent local fishing guides.

Mount Hutt Ski Area has the longest and most reliable ski season in New Zealand, and offers a "snow guarantee." Snow conditions range from powder in early winter to corn in late spring. 75 percent of the skiing terrain of its huge basin is rated "learner-intermediate," but advanced skiing in the back bowls is outstanding. Heliskiing is some of the best in the world.

Methven, the winter resort serving Mt. Hutt skifield (late May through early December), also operates as a base for moun-taineering, deer hunting and fishing. Within an hour's drive of Methven are three major rivers and numerous lakes. The Rakaia Gorge (100 miles RT), 10 miles north of Methven, is a very pic-turesque canyon. Follow Highway 72 to Darfield via scenic Glentunnel, returning to Christchurch via the Main West Road.

DAY 14
CHRISTCHURCH—QUEENSTOWN

Drive from Christchurch through alpine foothills over Burke's Pass to glacial lakes mirroring Mt. Cook National Park's mountains. Pass through only a handful of vacation villages in Mackenzie Valley, catering to skiers and sportsmen, then over the winding Lindis Pass road down to magnificent vistas of the Queenstown area.

Suggested Schedule

7:00 a.m.	Breakfast and check out.
7:30 a.m.	Rent a car for the drive around South Island and depart for Mt. Cook.
12:00 noon	Lunch in Mt. Cook Village.
1:00 p.m.	Walk from the village, scenic drive and walk to Blue Lakes (or) flightseeing to Tasman Glacier.
2:30 p.m.	Leave for Lake Ohau.
4:00 p.m.	Refreshments at the Ohau Lodge.
4:30 p.m.	Leave for Lindis Pass and Queenstown.
7:30 p.m.	Arrive in Queenstown and check in.
8:30 p.m.	Dinner. Stroll around the Queenstown Mall and lakefront.

Christchurch to Mt. Cook

The South Canterbury and North Otego provinces are separated by the Waitaki River, paralleled by Highways 83 and, from Kurow, Highway 82 linking Lake Benmore, New Zealand's largest man-made lake, to Oamaru and the east coast. Both provinces in this region look much alike: prosperous farming lands, vivid green in spring and brown at the end of summer.

Driving south across sheep-covered plains from Christchurch to Timaru is a monotonous 2½-hour trip, usually best seen from the air as a pattern of pastures, farmland, rivers and streams ascending foothills to the Alps. The same is true of the 1½-hour trip from Timaru south to Oamaru. Instead, leave Highway 1 at Geraldine for Highway 79, through Fairlie, Burke's Pass and beautiful Lake Pukaki, a deep milky blue from glacial minerals. Then turn north on Highway 80, paralleling Lake Pukaki to Mt. Cook. From there it's a a four-hour drive to Queenstown on Highway 8 through the Mackenzie Basin over the bleak tussock-covered hills of Lindis Pass.

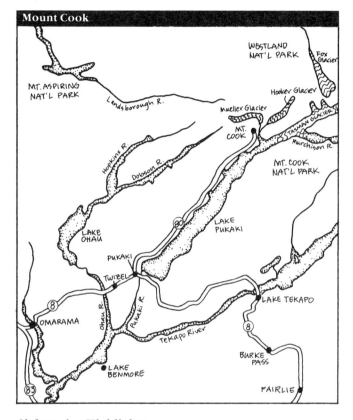

Mount Cook

WESTLAND NAT'L PARK

Fox Glacier

MT. ASPIRING NAT'L PARK

Landsborough R.

Hooker Glacier

Mueller Glacier

TASMAN GLACIER

MT. COOK

Murchison R.

Hopkins R.

Dobson R.

MT. COOK NAT'L PARK

LAKE OHAU

80

LAKE PUKAKI

PUKAKI

TWIZEL

Ohau R.

Pukaki R.

LAKE TEKAPO

8

OMARAMA

Tekapo River

8

LAKE BENMORE

BURKE PASS

83

FAIRLIE

Sightseeing Highlights

▲▲▲**Mount Cook** is the highest mountain in New Zealand (12,349 feet), surrounded by 140 peaks over 7000 feet. Between the mountains are glaciers, including the Tasman (18 miles long and two miles wide), the largest outside of the Himalayas and Antarctica. In winter, Mt. Cook offers excellent skiing: glacier, heli-skiing, alpine, nordic and ski mountaineering. Walkers, hikers and climbers will find the Mount Cook National Park to be a feast of scenery and native plants, including beautiful wildflowers from October to January. Stop at the Mt. Cook National Park Headquarters (tel. 818) in Mt. Cook Village for Park information.

Even a ten- to 30-minute walk from the village will reveal the park's great natural beauty. For a combination of a scenic drive and a short hike, take Highway 80 to Ball Hut Road, the Tasman

Valley Road, a gravel road that follows the Tasman River and
glacier to the carpark at Husky Flats. Follow the sign to Blue
Lakes and in 15 minutes you have a grand view of the lakes. A
few more minutes up the Clacker View Track for tremendous
views of Tasman Glacier, Mt. Tasman and Mt. Cook.

For hikers there are several excellent two- to 2½-hour walks:
Kea Point, Sealy Tarns and Red Tarns. The Hooker Valley Trail
leads over Copeland Pass to Fox Glacier (only for hikers with
alpine experience in ice and snow, the right equipment and a
guide). From Mt. Cook, light planes fly over the divide to Fox
and Franz Josef Glaciers. The Helicopter Line offers a 20-
minute cruise around Mt. Cook for NZ$50 and 45 minutes with
a snow landing for NZ$125 per person (tel. Mt. Cook 855). A
30-minute Mt. Cook Line flight landing on snow is NZ$100
(tel. Mt. Cook 849).

The Hermitage Hotel's travel desk (tel. 809) can book any activities in the area. Mount Cook Line buses connect with Christchurch (NZ$34) and Queenstown (NZ$34). Mount Cook Airlines fly in two or three times a day from Christchurch (NZ$125.40)
depending on the season. Newmans Airlines flies into Glentanner Airport (on the shores of Lake Pukaki, about 20 miles south
of the Village) from Christchurch, Wanaka and Queenstown (tel.
855 in Mt. Cook for latest schedules and fares).

A sumptuous smorgasbord lunch in the Alpine Room of the
world famous THC Hermitage (tel. 809), or a snack in the Coffee Bar, is something special to look forward to after the drive
from Christchurch. Stay at the THC-owned Mount Cook
Chalets (tel. 809), NZ$60 single or double, or the new YHA
Hostel (tel. 820) at NZ$12, if you find it too hard to leave the
Mount Cook area after just half a day.

▲**The Mackenzie Basin**'s vast tussock-covered expanses can
seem barren and monotonous in winter, but the dramatic
backdrop of the Southern Alps adds dramatic beauty to the trip.

▲▲**Lakes Tekapo and Pukaki** acquire blue-green and turquoise colors from fine dust created by glacial grinding that
feeds into their waters. In summer Lake Tekapo's shores are
covered with bluish purple, pink and yellow lupines. In winter
(July to late October) Lake Tekapo has a large beginners' ski area
and a ski school catering to novices. Nordic skiing on the
Hooker and Tasman Riverflats or on the glaciers and heliskiing
flights to the six- to eight-mile-long runs of the Tasman Glacier
are available from the local airfield. Contact Alpine Guides in
Mt. Cook (tel. 834) or Alpine Recreation Canterbury in Lake
Tekapo (tel. 736) for latest information, costs and bookings.

▲▲**Lake Ohau** west on Highway 8 between Twizel and Omarama, 1½ hours from Mt. Cook, is a beautiful place for fishing,
boating, hiking and skiing. Nearby Mt. Sutton has superb

heliski runs. Below the mountain, Lake Ohau Lodge provides luxury accommodations at only NZ$60 double. Nearby Oma-

Where to Stay: Queenstown

The **YHA Hostel**, 80 Esplanade, tel. 352, is well worth booking way in advance to ensure one of the best low-budget (NZ$8) lakeside accommodations in the world, assuming that you don't mind the curfew. The next best choices for budgeteers are: cabins, NZ$18 depending on facilities, or campsites in the **Queenstown Holiday Park**, tel. 29-306, at Arthur's Point; tourist flats (NZ$38-$50 two persons) or campsites in the **Queenstown Motor Park**, tel. 27-254, and the **Mountain View Lodge Holiday Park**, Frankton Rd., tel. 28-246, primarily a motel but with upper and lower tentsites, NZ$36 for two persons; and in Frankton, cabins, NZ$20-$30 for two persons, tent or caravan sites at the **Frankton Motor Camp**, tel. 27-247, and **Kawarau Falls Holiday Camp**, tel. 27-323.

The **Aroha Flats**, 20 Hay St., tel. 27-777, three minutes walk from the mall, with very spacious rooms and picture-postcard views of town and the lake, charging only NZ$39 for two persons is one of the best values in Queenstown. If you have a car, the **Lake Hayes Motel**, Lakes Hayes Rd., tel. AW705, literally on the shores of beautiful Lake Hayes, is a wonderful respite spot at NZ$47 for two persons.

A notch up in budget, B&B at NZ$48 for two persons, the **Wakatipu Lodge**, in Frankton at 25 Stewart St., tel. 23-037, has free shuttle service to Queenstown. For a location not too far from the center of town, with views and full facilities, the **Goldfields Guesthouse B&B**, 41 Frankton Rd., tel. 27-211, is a bargain at NZ$49-$54 for two persons. If these units are gone, ask about their B&B motel flats at NZ$58 for two persons.

The **Mountain View Lodge**, tel. 28-246, on Frankton Road competes with these prices, NZ$58 for two persons. Many other good motels are in the same price category, including the **Alpine Village Motor Inn**, Frankton Road, tel. 27-795, with great lakeside views, heated pools and a shuttle service; the **Four Seasons Motel**, 12 Standley St., tel. 28-953; the **Holloways Motel**, Lake Esplanade, tel. 28-589; and the **Modern Motel**, 8-12 Glasgow St., tel. 28-002, which matches views with the best; the very pretty **A-1 Queenstown Motel**, 13 Frankton Rd., tel. 27-289 with a private spa pool; and **Amber Motor Lodge**, Shotover St., tel. 28-480.

In the luxury category, the **Travelodge**, Beach St., tel. 27-800, may have captured the best location in town, but for better value for the money, NZ$145-$165, **The Lofts**, tel. 27-391, a condominium on nearby Shotover Street, offers class, comfort and intimacy.

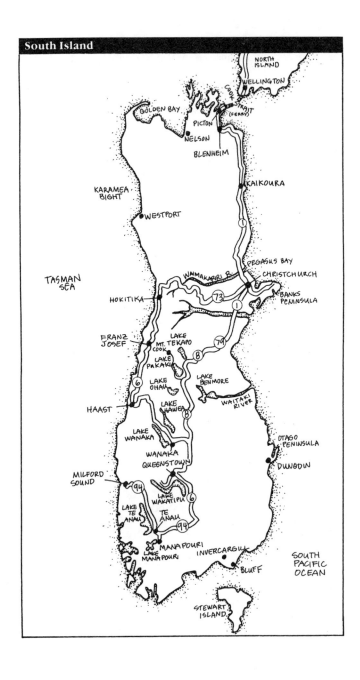

Itinerary Options: Dunedin—Otago Peninsula—Stewart Island

Dunedin and the Otago Peninsula is an itinerary option requiring at least three days of driving and touring time between Christchurch and Queenstown. There is no direct way to drive from Dunedin to Queenstown, only Dunedin-Ranfurly-Alexandra-Cromwell-Queenstown or Dunedin-Milton-Raes Junction-Alexandra-Cromwell-Queenstown. Either route requires a six-hour drive.

Dunedin: Fueled by Central Otago's gold rush in the 1860s, Dunedin became Victorian New Zealand's wealthiest town. "The Edinburgh of the South" envisioned by its Scottish founders flourished as a planned city with more interesting, diverse architecture than any other in the country. Dunedin is framed by a greenbelt on the hills facing the harbor set between the rugged Otago Peninsula and the coast.

North of the City, Signal Hill and Mount Cargill offer sweeping panoramas of the harbor, or follow the four-mile Queens Drive through the Town Belt. Other viewpoints include Unity Park, Bracken's Lookout, Southern Cemetery and Prospect Park.

The 35-room Jacobean-style Olveston Mansion, Dunedin's primary attraction, is a showcase of European antiques only matched by the Larnarch Castle on Otago Peninsula.

The Otago Peninsula: This is the third of New Zealand's extraordinary peninsulas, the others being Coromandel and Banks. The Otago Peninsula, northeast of Dunedin, offers high-contrast scenery between the Otago Harbour and Pacific Ocean sides: serene and dotted with settlements on the harbor side, wild and rugged on the ocean side.

Larnach Castle (1871), a 43-room neo-gothic "monument" set in 35 acres of gardens, contains a 3000 sq. ft. ballroom crafted and furnished in grand style. Richly carved ceilings and Venetian glass, created by imported European craftsmen, decorate the rooms. The Tower, over 1000 feet above sea-level, provides superb views of the Peninsula and harbor.

The Royal Albatross Colony is the closest nesting place to a developed area for these huge birds. The breeding grounds can be visited with prior arrangement, from November through September, with December to May the best viewing months. Chicks hatch in January.

Yellow-eyed penguins come ashore to nest in Penguin Bay and seals bask on a rocky islet (Seal Island) only 10 yards from shore.

Stewart Island: You need a good reason for driving the 3 ½ hours from Dunedin to Invercargill (plus as least three more hours if you follow the southeastern coastal route). For nature lovers, the very good reason is Stewart Island.

From Bluff on the ferry *MV Wairua*, Stewart Island is two hours across the Foveaux Strait (or 20 minutes by air). With its brilliant dawns and sunsets, the Maoris call it Rakiura—"Island of the Glowing Sky." Most of the 500 people on this un-spoiled 40-mile by 25-mile (425,000 acre) island, descendants of European whalers, live in Halfmoon Bay (Oban) and fish the often stormy Pacific and Antarctic waters. Visit the Rakiura Museum for Stewart Island's history.

With only 12½ miles of road on the northern coast, this is an island for walkers, bird-watchers, and deer hunters. Bring waterproof clothing and boots. In particular, this island is an or-nithologist's paradise: tui and bellbirds in spring, tomtit and rare wekas in summer, fantails in winter, and parakeets, kakas, fernbirds, dottrels, brown creepers, moreporks, and perhaps even kiwis year-round.

Launch cruise charters and self-charters visit Ulva Island's sandy beaches and wooded walking trails, Paterson Inlet, Ocean Beach, Port Adventure and Port William. Enjoy short walks to Horeshoe Bay, Garden Mound, Ringoringa Beach and Lee Bay. The northern part of the island offers weeks of hiking, but obtain local information and maps first, and avoid wander-ing off the beaten track.

The **South Sea Hotel** (tel. 6), a B&B for NZ$35, **Rakiura Motel** (tel. 27S) at NZ$45 for two persons, **Horseshoe Haven**'s (tel. 56K) A-frame units at NZ$31 for two and a lodge at NZ$11 per person, and **Ferndale Caravan Park** (tel. 52M) at NZ$35 for two persons are all the accommodations you'll find on the island except for forestry huts, a few campsites, and private homes that make room available to vacationers.

DAY 15
QUEENSTOWN

Board the *S.S. Earnslaw* for a mid-morning cruise on Lake
Wakatipu to a lakeside working sheep station. After returning to
Queenstown, visit Arrowtown for lunch as a leisurely start for a
memorably exciting afternoon of jetboating on the Shotover
River and backcountry four-wheeling, or possibly horse trek-
king, to catch the sunset.

Suggested Schedule

8:00 a.m.	Lakeside snack breakfast. Sightseeing and shopping on the Queenstown Mall.
10:00 a.m.	*S.S. Earnslaw* cruise (with more breakfast) to Mt. Nicholas Sheep Station.
12:00 noon	Drive or bus to Arrowtown for sightseeing and lunch, with a side trip up Coronet Peak for the view.
3:00 p.m.	Shotover jetboat trip.
8:00 p.m.	Dinner and relaxation on Bob's Peak. Spend the night in Queenstown or Frankton.

Orientation

Queenstown is the South Island's, New Zealand's and one of
the world's most outstanding recreational resorts. The variety
of spectacular year-round lake, mountain and river recreational
attractions in the region, including Queenstown, Te Anau,
Fiordland National Park, Wanaka and Mt. Aspiring National
Park, is unsurpassed anywhere. Nestled at the head of a small
bay on Lake Wakatipu (52 miles long), surrounded by rugged
mountains rising steeply from the shoreline, Queenstown is a
compact village easily toured on foot. Using Queenstown as a
base, after arriving you can book a seemingly unlimited variety
of excursions: whitewater rafting, jetboats, cruise trips, hydrofoil
rides, four wheel drive and horse-back trips, climbing, hiking
back-country camping, skiing (mostly downhill and heliskiing),
fishing, and combinations thereof, with guides and helicopter
transport options, from a half-day to a week or more.
 The more popular excursions fill rapidly, especially during
peak tourist months, so be prepared to make booking decisions
as soon as you arrive in town. The NZTP Travel Office (tel. 143)
on Shotover Street can fill all your information and booking requirements for lake and river trips, horseback trips, flightseeing

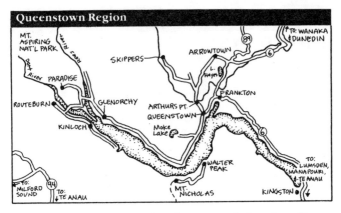

excursions to Milford Sound, and accommodations from Te Anau to Wanaka.

Sightseeing Highlights

▲▲▲**Lake Wakatipu** deserves a leisurely cruise or launch trip for one to three hours. The *S.S. Earnslaw*, a completely renovated coal-burning steam ship that made her debut on the lake in 1912, sails several times a day (NZ$19 adult, NZ$9.50 child) to the Mt. Nicholas Sheep Station for a sheep shearing demonstration. Cross the lake by launch (NZ$17 adult, NZ$8.50 child) to the Cecil Peak Sheep and Cattle Station (soon to have a major resort development). The hydrofoil *Meteor III* takes passengers on a 25-mile cruise to the upper reaches of the lake (NZ$22 adult, NZ$11 child) and offers a 20-minute mini-cruise (NZ$10 adult, NZ$7.50 child).

▲▲▲**The Shotover and Kawarau Rivers** offer the ultimate in white-water rafting and jetboat experiences. Jetboat from Queenstown down the lake to the Kawarau River and then downriver. Shoot incredible white-water rapids through the narrow canyon of the Shotover River and then raft through the Upper Kawarau. Rafting trips range from NZ$40 to NZ$90 per person, jetboat trips NZ$30 adult, NZ$15 child. Helicopter flights will take you to and from the rivers on flightseeing trips and even drop you off at the top of Bob's Peak (NZ$85 per person). White-water hovercraft trips are available for those who would rather wisk through the foaming rapids on a cushion of air in an enclosed cabin (NZ$50 per person).

▲▲**Arrowtown** is a pretty village of old wood and stone cottages nestling beneath Sycamore trees, the relic of a gold mining boom that brought thousands of miners to the Arrow and Shotover Rivers. The Lake District Centennial Museum in

Arrowtown contains one of the country's best gold-mining sections.

▲▲**Coronet Peak**, 12 miles north of Queenstown on the way to Arrowtown, has a chair-lift to the summit station for a magnificent panoramic view of Lake Wakatipu and the Southern Alps. In winter, from mid-June to October, Coronet Peak and the Remarkables give Queenstown two of the most challenging skiing terrains in the Southern Hemisphere. Even if you don't ski, the views of surrounding mountains and lakes from the Remarkables' access road is worth the trip (put on chains in the winter).

▲▲**Bob's Peak** and its Skyline Restaurant, reached by a four-minute (1,530-foot) gondola ride (NZ$5.50 adult, NZ$1.50 child) starting near the town center, is the best and easiest way to see the town and its surroundings on a clear day or night.

Where to Eat

After a day of jetboating, whitewater rafting or other adventuresome and vigorous activity, any food will look and smell great. Add a touch of ambience, charm or a roaring fireplace on a cool night and it can seem brilliant. Restaurants in Queenstown that qualify for this description are: pizzas and spaghetti dishes at the cozy **Cow Restaurant**, tel. 567, on Cow Lane; **Sablis**, Arcade on Beach Street, tel. 145, for a wide variety of meat and fowl dishes; **Upstairs Downstairs**, 66 Shotover Street, tel. 203; and next door, New Zealand's traditional meat and fowl cuisine at **Roaring Megs**, 57 Shotover St., tel. 968, with candlelight and some dress-up. You shouldn't miss eating, drinking or both at the **Skyline**, tel. 123, on Bob's Peak in Queenstown, reached by cable car. The food may not be remarkable, but the view is.

By and large, stick to tasty budget meals in Queenstown, such as **Twenty Minutes** in the mall, the **Gourmet Express Restaurant and Coffee Shop** in the Bay Centre on Shotover Street, the **Rees Cafe** in Rees Place Arcade and the **Remarkable Food Establishment** on Rees Street, and **Cobb & Co.**, Rees and Beach Streets.

Westy's on the Mall, tel. 609, serves excellent food at inflated prices. **Packer's Arms**, tel. 929, is a very expensive dining "experience" in an historic building on Arthur's Point. If you get cold feet, try **Arthur's Point Pub and Restaurant** for scafood or steaks and nightly specials.

The Flash in the Pan, The Mall, Buckingham St., tel. 828, in Arrowtown serves a decent lunch.

Itinerary Options

Skippers Canyon is about four hours round-trip by mini-coach

or four-wheel-drive vehicle from Queenstown (NZ$26.50
adult, NZ$13 child). The narrow, single-lane road that snakes
high above the Shotover River is unforgettable, especially on a
winter trip! A three-hour horseback trip up the Shotover and
Moonlight Valleys leaves at 9:30 a.m. and 2:00 p.m. from
Moonlight Stables, NZ$28.50. A three-hour ride through Ar-
row River Gorge from **Hunters Horse Trekking** leaves at the
same times and costs the same.

DAY 16
QUEENSTOWN—TE ANAU

Te Anau, near the southern end of the largest of the region's lakes, is the gateway and touring base for excursions to Milford and Doubtful Sounds and Lake Manapouri. The 120-mile trip from Queenstown on Highways 6 and 94 through Lumsden and sheep and cattle country should take no more than three hours.

Suggested Schedule

7:00 a.m.	Early breakfast in Queenstown.
8:00 a.m.	Check out and leave for Te Anau.
11:00 a.m.	Check in at Te Anau. Confirm Milford and other bookings.
12:00 noon	Picnic Lunch at Lake Te Anau.
1:00 p.m.	Half-day launch trip to West Arm.
6:30 p.m.	Leisurely dinner and early to bed.

Sightseeing Highlights
▲▲▲**Fiordland National Park**, New Zealand's largest and most remote park, covers over three million acres of the southwestern South Island. Take the main road out of Queenstown to Frankton, then south on Highway 6 along the Remarkables through Kingston to just before Lumsden, where Highway 94 branches west to the towns of Te Anau and Manapouri, just outside the park's boundary, and Fiordland National Park. Gaze in wonderment at the still waters of deep glacier-formed fiords broken only by seals, dolphins and penguins. Towering waterfalls tumble from sheer 4500-foot walls. Mountain peaks reflect in deep blue lakes dotted with forest-covered islands. Crystal clear rivers, powered by seemingly endless days of rain or drizzle, flow from rugged, snow-capped and often mist-shrouded mountains covered with dense green beech forests that shelter the blue and iridescent green takahe and the nocturnal, flightless kiwi, weka and kakapo, some of the world's rarest birds. These unique sightseeing experiences are unsurpassed anywhere on earth, even on gloomy, overcast Fiordland days. Winter—June to August—is the best time for clear views and relatively little rain. The road to Milford is open in winter, but the higher elevations are subject to heavy snowfalls. In summer, prepare (with your favorite insect repellant) for the fly in the Fiordland's ointment: tiny ferocious black sandflies that inflict painful, itchy bites, especially around dusk.

▲▲**Lake Manapouri**, which tends to be overlooked in relation
to Lake Wakatipu and Te Anau, may be New Zealand's most
beautiful lake, as well as the deepest (1500 feet). The lake contains 30 picturesque islets. Stockyard Cove is a lovely spot for
picnics. Take a launch tour to the West Arm to visit the hydro-
electric powerhouse 700 feet under a mountain. Water from the
Lake plunges through turbines and then along a six-mile tunnel
into Doubtful Sound. From the tunnel a bus travels over the
2200 foot Wilmot Pass to Deep Cove. Then board a two-hour
launch cruise on Doubtful Sound, ten times larger than Milford
Sound, with waterfalls cascading hundreds of feet. A full-day's
coach trip, including the cruise, costs NZ$55.

Where to Stay
Budget travelers will appreciate Te Anau's **YHA Hostel**, Milford
Rd., tel. 7847, one of the most attractive in New Zealand, about
a mile from town (NZ$8).
   Inexpensive camping sites and cabins are available at various
distances from Te Anau. The **Mountain View Cabin and
Caravan Park** has cabins for NZ$18 for 2 persons. **Te Anau
Motor Park**, Manapouri Highway, tel. 7457, about one-half
mile from town, costs NZ$5 per person and also has cabins and
chalets, NZ$17-$48 for two persons, and caravan sites. Outside
of Manapouri, 12 miles south of Te Anau, the **Lakeview Motor
Park**, Te Anau Rd., tel. 624, has cabins at NZ$18 for two per-
sons; and, on a beautiful lakeside site, the **Manapouri Glade
Caravan Park**'s cabins charge NZ$15 for two persons, tel. 623.
   Among B&Bs, the **Matai Lodge**, Matai St., tel. 7360, is one of
the few with doubles under NZ$50. Among motels, only the
XL Motel, Te Anau Tce., tel. 7258, has rates under NZ$50 for
doubles. There are numerous motels in the NZ$50-$60 range.

Where to Eat
Considering the number of tourists heading for Milford Sound,
Te Anau could use more eating places in budget- and medium-
price categories. Except for those that may be opening as I'm
writing, the choices for decent and down-home, nothing-fancy
fare include: the **Coffee Shop** on Main Street; **Vacation Inn**,
The Gallery; the **Luxmore Motor Lodge** on Milford Road, and
Bailey's next door; **Light Bight** on the lakefront; and **Pop-in
Catering** on Te Anau Terrace for breakfasts and hot meals. The
only somewhat fancier and higher-priced eating place is the
Grubsteak Restaurant at the THC Te Anau Hotel on Te Anau
Terrace.

Itinerary Options
Take a ten-minute helicopter flight to Mt. Luxmore and over

Lake Manapouri for NZ$35 or one of a dozen other chopper and floatplane trips over the region at prices that start at NZ$25 per person up to NZ$200. **Air Fiordland** (tel. 7505), **Waterwings Airways** (tel. 7405) or **Fiordland Flights** (tel. 7799) will arrange these flights and pick you up in Te Anau, or you can drive out to the Te Anau Airfield south of town.

Hiking and Skiing in the Southern Alps
Fiordland National Park and Mount Aspiring National Park contain incredibly beautiful terrain, both tame and wild. The rugged, snow-capped mountain ranges, dense rain forests, alpine lakes and rivers, waterfalls and majestic fiords, offer a marvelous variety of "tramping" experiences of varying difficulties. Accessed from Te Anau and Queenstown, the Milford Track, Routeburn Walk, Hollyford Valley Walk and Greenstone Valley Walk range from difficult to easy and none requires more than good physical fitness, comfortable and waterproof gear, and adequate time. Experienced independent "trampers" hike these trails all the time with track and weather information supplied by national park offices. Various tour operators in the region provide guides, transportation, meals, camping equipment and accommodation arrangements for small groups in a competent but delightfully easygoing manner.

The Milford Track, a 35-mile trail, is New Zealand's best known walk. Highlights of the track are views from MacKinnon Pass, the 1800-foot Sutherland Falls, the incredible variety of rain forest, and the torrents of water cascading everywhere after rain.

With an early morning departure to Te Anau from Queenstown, the Milford Track round-trip takes five days (including an arrival day in Queenstown). Open from early November to early April, a permit is necessary from the Park Headquarters in Te Anau. For independent hikers, an NZRR bus leaves Te Anau for the 45-minute ride to Te Anau Downs at 1:15 p.m., connecting with the boat to Glade House. Each of the next three days of walking is divided into 10 to 13 mile segments, followed by hot showers and meals at Pompolona Lodge and then Quintin Hut. At the end of the trail, a boat leaves Sandfly Point at 2:00 p.m. and 4:00 p.m. for Milford. If you do not plan to catch the 3:00 p.m. bus to Te Anau, know that the next bus leaves at 7:45 a.m.

The Hollyford Valley Walk is a way to combine tramping, river jet-boating and flightseeing to Milford Sound, the scenic drive from Milford to Te Anau, and fishing for trout and kahawai. From late October to mid-April, tramp along the broad Hollyford Valley to the Tasman Sea at Martin's Bay (four-day trip), departing on a scenic flight to Milford Sound or

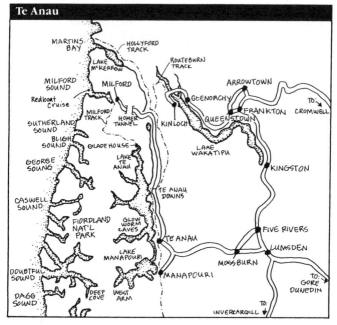

flightsee over Milford and Routeburn tracks; or a five-day trip
alternative including a jet-boat on Lake McKerrow. Contact
Hollyford Tourist & Travel Ltd., Invercargill, tel. 44300. The
walk in/walk-out tour is 24 miles; walk in/fly-out is 16 miles;
with optional sidetrips of another 12 miles; or 55 miles of a jet-
boating option. For a much easier walk than Milford or Hollyford, the 22-mile Greenstone Valley Walk has much to offer.
The trail passes beautiful lakes Howden and McKellar, then
follows the Greenstone River to Lake Wakatipu. Greenstone is
one of the walks that can be done all year but October through
April is the best time. Much less well known than the Milford
Track, the Routeburn Walk is nonetheless one of the best rain
forest/sub-alpine trails in the world. Spanning two magnificent
national parks, the 25-mile trail starts and finishes about 1500
feet above sea level, with a great variety of scenery and flora.
Highlights of the trip are views from Harris Saddle (4200 feet)
and Key Summit. The higher elevations mostly eliminate the
sandfly problem that plagues the Milford Track. The keen
tramper can combine a Hollyford and Routeburn walk. Often
the Greenstone Walk is used as the return to Queenstown from
Routeburn. At Elfin Bay you can charter a jet-boat to Queenstown or walk to Kinloch to meet the bus to Routeburn.
Routeburn Walk Ltd., Queenstown, tel. 100, offers a guided

walk, with transportation from Queenstown, accommodations and meals, for about NZ$350 per adult. An advantage of this tour is that Routeburn Falls and Lake Mackenzie Lodges are available exclusively for this tour.

Skiing in the Southern Alps: The scenery is stunningly beautiful and virtually unmarked by resort or other development. The ski lifts and slopes are comparatively uncrowded. Waiting at lifts is uncommon. You spend most of your time skiing, even on weekends. With a favorable currency exchange rate, lift tickets, equipment rentals, excellent ski instruction, accommodations, and apres-ski activities cost about half as much as in the US. Returning from the ski mountains, if there's time you can engage in virtually all of the other year-round activities mentioned above. Sounds too good to be true? Except for very rare lack of snow, in the Queenstown-Wanaka region it's all true.

Close to Queenstown, Coronet Peak has excellent skiing at all levels, especially advanced and intermediate, with one of the best ski schools in New Zealand. Lift tickets are interchangeable with the Remarkables. The Remarkables have more excellent beginner and intermediate trails than Coronet. There are Nordic ski trails above the lifts and telemark instruction is available.

The Harris Mountains are New Zealand's leading heliskiing area with over 140 runs from 40 different peaks in three mountain ranges. Experienced and advanced skiers can have 12,000 feet of awe-inspiring runs in the Tyndall Glaciers and Buchanan Range. The cost is about NZ$350 per day or about NZ$16 per 1000 vertical feet.

Treble Cone, 18 miles from Wanaka, deserves to be much better known for its skiing and scenery. A skier chalet at the top of the double chairlift offers spectacular views of surrounding mountains. Many of the Harris Mountain heliskiing trips begin from Treble Cone. Cardrona is the South Island's most promising new ski area. A high base elevation (4500 feet) and southerly exposure provide ample snow coverage in the June-November season.

DAY 17
TE ANAU—MILFORD SOUND

Start very early on a full-day round-trip from Te Anau to
fabulous Milford Sound, including a three-hour drive over The
Divide and through Homer Tunnel to the end of the road at
THC Milford Resort Hotel, then a cruise through Milford Sound
to see pyramid-shaped Mitre Peak, Stirling Falls and several
other magnificent waterfalls arching into the sound from high
sheer walls and hanging valleys.

Suggested Schedule

7:00 a.m.	Breakfast in Te Anau.
8:30 a.m.	Drive to Milford Sound with sightseeing stops at lakes along the way.
12:00 noon	Lunch Cruise on Milford Sound.
2:30 p.m.	Return to Te Anau.
3:00 p.m.	Te Ana-au Caves Tour.
5:00 p.m.	Return to Te Anau for an early dinner.

Transportation
Te Anau to Milford Sound is a three-hour drive by way of Eglinton and Hollyford Valleys and Homer Tunnel. It's 60 miles
through beech forests surrounded by high rugged peaks. The
high rainfall creates dark green beech forests covering thick
fern, shrub, rich carpets of spongy moss and peat, and other
plant growth, even on steep rock faces. Start driving early to
Milford on Highway 94 (Milford Road) to beat the mountains
clouding up or bad weather. A call to Park Headquarters (tel.
7521) at 8:00 a.m. for the weather report would be sensible. Be
sure to wear or bring waterproof and warm gear. The first 18
miles of the road skirts the shores of Lake Te Anau, then follows
the Englinton River flanked by beech forests. On the way
through Englinton Valley to The Divide, the 1500-foot pass over
the Southern Alps, Mirror Lakes (about 25 miles), beautiful Lake
Gunn (about 50 miles) are worthwhile stopping places. Although little more than ponds, Mirror Lakes yield perfect reflections of surrounding peaks. Climb the forested ridge to Cascade
Creek which, in addition to accommodations and refreshments, has views of many waterfalls cascading from bush-
covered valley walls. Then drive over The Divide, eight miles
before Homer Tunnel, the starting point of the Routeburn and
Greenstone tracks to Lake Wakatipo. From Hollyford Road to

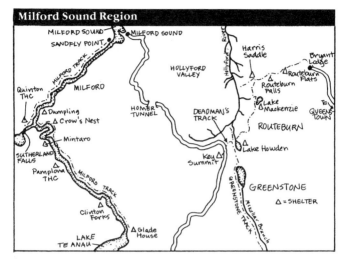

Homer Tunnel, pass through the beech forest and tussock river flats of Hollyford Valley, some of the best scenery on the trip. Named after Harry Homer, who discovered the Homer Saddle in 1889, the 3600-foot-long Homer Tunnel, begun in 1935, wasn't completed until 1953. The eastern entrance to Homer Tunnel is 8100 feet in elevation, descending through the tunnel to 2700 feet. The Cleddau Valley at the far end of the tunnel was carved through rock by the raging waters of the Cleddau River. At the end of the Milford trip, through the Cleddau Valley, is a one-to-two hour Milford Sound launch cruise with fabulous views of Mitre Peak and Sutherland Falls.

NZRRS and Fiordland Travel run regular bus services from Te Anau for NZ$13 one way or NZ$20 round-trip. The coach excursion leaves at 8:15 a.m. and returns at 5:45 p.m. Both the THC and Fiordland Travel operate launch trips on Milford Sound. With a lunch on board, the longer cruise costs NZ$20.

One option to consider is Te Anau-Milford by bus and return by air to either Te Anau or Queenstown. Fly with Mt. Cook Airlines (NZ$80 per adult) or take a short flight to the mouth of the sound for NZ$30.

Sightseeing Highlight

▲▲**Lake Te Anau**, branching into three land-locked fiords, offers an ideal introduction to the region's thickly wooded mountains. Set on glacier-gouged Lake Te Anau, the South Island's largest lake has a backdrop of the Kepler Mountains and the Murchison Range running parallel to the north. "Te Anau" is a short version of a Maori word, *Te Ana-Au*, meaning "caves of rushing waters." The myriad mysterious shapes of greenish glowworms gleaming from 15,000 years of limestone accretions have made these recently discovered caves across the lake one of the most popular local attractions. Te Ana-Au Caves can only be reached by boat, costing NZ$21 adult, NZ$8 child. Book this 2½ hour round trip at the Fiordland Travel Centre (at the intersection of Milford Road and Te Anau Terrace, tel. 7416) which, besides Park Headquarters, is the main source of travel information for the Te Anau-Manapouri-Milford Sound area. While you're there, pick up NZ$.50 tokens to visit the Te Anau Underground Trout Observatory, south along Te Anau Terrace across from Park Headquarters, where you can watch, feed and photograph brown, rainbow and native trout daily from 6:00 a.m. to 9:45 p.m. To find some easy walks along the lake, from the observatory continue south on Te Anau Terrace and turn right on the road along the lake toward Manapouri. Starting at the control gates, Riverside Walk and several extensions offer one- to five-hour one-way walks of varying difficulty around the lake, up Mt. Luxmore and to Lake Manapouri.

▲▲▲**Milford Sound**—Cruise down the ten-mile-long, deeply furrowed glacial trough hemmed in by rock walls reaching from 900 feet underwater to almost a mile high. This fiord to the Tasman Sea passes Mitre Peak, from its reflection in the dark waters soaring over 5000 feet straight out of the sound; passes close enough to 450-foot Stirling Falls to feel the spray, and also Bowen Falls cascading about 500 feet from a hanging valley over two or three tiers. Watch for dolphins, seals lying on Seal Point's rocks, and Fiordland crested penguins. From the hotel, it's just a short walk up a flight of steps to Look-out Track for excellent views of the sound, or continue further up a steep ridge for higher viewpoints.

Accommodations

Book well ahead at the **THC Milford Hostel** if you plan to stay overnight at Milford Sound (NZ$14). The only other choice, at the head of the Fiord, is the luxurious **THC Milford Resort Hotel**, which owns the territory and charges NZ$125-$150 double for the privilege of enjoying the utterly unique environment in a first-rate hotel, worth it if your budget allows.

DAY 18
TE ANAU-QUEENSTOWN-WANAKA

Leave Te Anau early in order to take Highway 89 from Queenstown to Wanaka and still have an active day of hiking, boating and fishing in the Lake Wanaka area.

Suggested Schedule

7:00 a.m.	Breakfast and check out.
10:30 a.m.	Highway 89 to Wanaka.
12:30 p.m.	Lunch in Wanaka.
1:30 p.m.	Walk up Mt. Iron.
2:30 p.m.	Glendhu Bay and boat trip on Lake Wanaka, or Lake Hawea for trout fishing.
7:30 p.m.	Dinner at Ripples Restaurant.

Driving from Te Anau to Westland
Retrace your driving route on Highway 94 east to Lumstedn, then north on Highway 6 to Queenstown. Lake Wanaka is two hours from Queenstown. From Queenstown to Haast on the west coast through Wanaka is a six-hour drive.

In good weather only (not in mid-winter!), drive Highway 89 up the very steep unpaved road from Arrowtown to the top of the Crown Ridge for magnificent views overlooking Wakapitu Lake, the Kawarau River, Queenstown and the Remarkables. This road passes through Cardrona Valley from Wanaka to Queenstown, 44 miles of slow-going, bumpy unpaved road (versus 57 miles following Highway 6 around the Pisa Range).

Sightseeing Highlights
▲▲▲**Wanaka** is one of New Zealand's (and the world's) most underrated resorts because it is in the shadow of Queenstown, only 60 miles away. Lakes Wanaka and Hawea are famed for their fishing (brown and rainbow trout and land-locked salmon). It has the best weather and most sunshine days in the southern lakes. Many skiers from the U.S. and Europe prefer Treble Cone to Coronet Peak (Queenstown is still the apres-ski favorite). The Wanaka region has most of the same outdoor recreational choices as Queenstown. For panoramic views of Lake Wanaka and Mt. Aspiring National Park, walk up Mt. Roy (3 hours) or Mt. Iron (1 hour). From Wanaka's airfield (Mt. Aspiring Air) or from the waterfront take flightseeing excursions (NZ$20-$50) over the wilderness and lakes of Mt. Aspiring

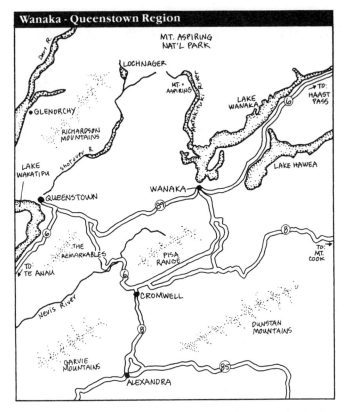

Wanaka - Queenstown Region

National Park, to Milford Sound (NZ$80) and even to Mt. Cook (NZ$125).

▲▲**Glendhu Bay**, west of Wanaka and Roy's Peak on Wanaka Aspiring Road, especially in autumn, is renowned for its seasonal beauty and views of Mt. Aspiring National Park.

Where to Stay

The **YHA Hostel**, 181 Upton St., tel. 7405, is central, comfortable and charges NZ$10. The next cheapest accommodations, also centrally located, are at the **Wanaka Motor Camp**'s cabins, 212 Brownstone St., tel. 7883, at NZ$30 for two persons. A favorite is the **Glendhu Bay Camp**, adjacent to Lake Wanaka, Treble Cone Rd., tel. 7243, also for NZ$33 for two persons. Less than two miles from Wanaka, **Pleasant Lodge Caravan Park**, Mt. Aspiring Rd., tel. 7360, has cabins at NZ$20 for two persons, as well as caravan rentals. Check out **Penrith**

Park's cabins, Beacon Point, tel. 7009, at NZ$18-$20 for two persons and bunkrooms in the lodge at NZ$35 for two persons.

There are only a few B&Bs, with first choice the **Wanaka Lodge**, 117 Lakeside Rd., tel. 7837, right on the lake with great views, for NZ$45 twin. The **Creekside Guest House**, 84 Helwick St., tel. 7834, also costs NZ$45 double.

The half dozen or more excellent local motels with self-contained units cost NZ$45-$60 for two persons. For one night, this may be the occasion when it is worth spending the extra few dollars at the **THC Wanaka**, tel. 7826, NZ$60-$90, very comfortable rooms with beautiful lake and mountain views.

Where to Eat
Like Te Anua, Wanaka lacks variety in budget and medium-priced restaurants. For lunch try a bistro meal at the **Storehouse Restaurant** or soup, salad and maybe pizza at **Te Kano Cafe**. **First Cafe** on Ardmore St. is very good but only open for dinner. The big surprise for dinner is little **Ripples Restaurant**, tel. 7413, in the Pembroke Mall, from appetizers to desserts a candidate for the prize BYO of the Southern Alps.

DAY 19

WANAKA TO FOX AND FRANZ JOSEF GLACIERS

Leave very early once more for an eight-hour drive (including stops) from Wanaka through the Makarora Valley to Haast Pass, descending to the two great glaciers of Westland National Park, Fox and Franz Josef. Thirteen miles apart, Fox and Franz Josef Glaciers descend about six miles into rain forests 1000 feet above sea level. The land rises to peaks over 10,000 feet high with incredible scenery. Today and tomorrow, take advantage of fabulous recreational opportunities, including glacier excursions and forest walks at both glaciers.

Suggested Schedule

7:00 a.m.	Breakfast and check out.
8:00 a.m.	Depart for Haast Pass.
12:00 noon	Picnic lunch near Haast Pass.
2:30 p.m.	Arrive Fox Glacier.
3:00 p.m.	Climb to Fox Chalet Lookout for sunset views.
6:30 p.m.	Head for Franz Josef to check in, dine and relax in front of a fireplace.

Wanaka to Fox and Franz Josef Glaciers
The Haast Pass Road (Highway 6) from Wanaka to Westland National Park passes through fabulous scenery. With many one-lane bridges and gravel sections, steep slopes, blind and sharp corners, magnificent scenery and viewpoints, walking and picnicking opportunities, you can't hurry—and don't want to.

From Wanaka, continue to follow Highway 6, first along Lake Hawea and then along Lake Wanaka up the Makarora River Valley to Haast Pass. Drive through Mt. Aspiring National Park, named for the highest and most magnificent peak (over 10,000 feet), and over Haast Pass (1700 feet). Mount Cook is only 50 miles to the north.

Highway 6 skirts the western shore of Lake Hawea, another scenic gem known for its trout and land-locked salmon fishing, then crosses The Neck between Lakes Hawea and Wanaka, and follows Lake Wanaka to Makarora Gorge. One of the most scenic parts of the entire trip lies in Mt. Aspiring National Park, between the Gorge and Haast Pass. The mountain after which the park is named rises 10,000 feet west of Wanaka. Along Highway 6 to the 1500-foot pass, the Makaroa and other rivers flow in and out of hills and flats covered with sheep, with snow-capped peaks in the background.

From the pass, the Haast River drops through the gorge known as the Gates of Haast, where it roars through a gorge full of enormous boulders. The river is joined by the larger Landsborough in a wider valley along which you can drive down to the sea. You may want to stop in Haast, refuel and stock up on food supplies before continuing. Cross Haast Bridge and travel north 15 miles to Knights Point, a headland fringed by golden sand beaches and rocky bays, where you may see seals playing offshore just south of Lake Hoeraki, with glacial lake water and good fishing. Other good stops are two lake gems: Lake Moeraki and Lake Paringa.

Sightseeing Highlights

▲▲▲**Westland National Park**—Fox and Franz Josef Glaciers are unique in that they push steeply down into rain forest within a few miles of the sea. The park contains over 60 named glaciers and beautiful lakes. Fox and Franz Josef Glaciers can be visited easily from the Westland National Park Visitor Centres. To get to Fox Glacier from the village, backtrack south on Highway 6 a little over a mile to the Glacier Access Road. Watch for the Glacier View Road sign on the right. At the south end of Glacier View Road starts the 40-minute (one-way) Chalet Lookout Track. The Cone Rock Track branches off the Chalet Lookout Track, climbing steeply 1000 feet above the Fox River, a strenuous hour on a steep switchback trail. The Chalet Lookout Track is much less strenuous. From Fox Glacier Hotel a walking track to lovely Minnehaha Creek is just a 20-minute stroll through forest. Try it at night with a flashlight to see thousands of glowworms dangling in the rain forest.

Tomorrow in Franz Josef, stop at the Park Centre for brochures on short walking tracks in the area and general information on hiking in the glaciers. Franz Josef Glacier is less than four miles from the Centre. Head back south along Highway 6 for a few hundred yards to the turnoff onto the Glacier Access Road. From this road through the rainforest, many tracks branch out for 30 minutes to three or four hours of moderate to strenuous walking. The Centre's brochures provide details on all of these tracks. Don't forget to bring rainwear and plenty of potent insect repellant in late spring and summer months. Tomorrow, also plan to see at least one of the beautiful nearby Lakes— Kaniere, Mapourika, Mahinapua, Mauapiurike, Matheson, Paring, Brunner, Ianthe or Wahapo.

Where to Stay

The cost of accommodations in the Franz Josef area is lower

than in the Southern Alps, but the supply can be very
short during the summer peak season. Book ahead.

There are some excellent choices for budget watchers. The
comparatively new **Franz Josef YHA Hostel**, Cron Street, tel.
745, costs NZ$10. The excellent **Franz Josef Motor Camp** on
the main road, tel. 766, has all facilities including a camp store,
with cabins at NZ$15 and cottages at NZ$21 for two persons.
Forks Motorcamp, Okarito, tel. Whataroa 351, 12 miles north,
is in a beautiful setting, but has only two units costing NZ$12
for two persons.

Except for the higher-priced **THC Franz Josef**, tel. 819, and
the centrally located **Westland Motor Inn**, main road, tel. 728,
NZ$75-$95 double, local motels with lovely settings, glacier
views and excellent facilites are NZ$50 and under: the **Glacier
View Motel**, tel. 705, **Bushland Court Motel**, Cron St., tel.
757, and **Motel Franz Josef**, main road, 3 miles north, tel. 742.

Where to Eat

Apart from a decent sandwich at Fox Glacier's **Hobnail Cafe** or
a light meal at the **Fox Glacier Hotel**, tel. 838, either buy and
cook your own food or save your appetite and money for Franz
Josef.

In Franz Josef, the best place for grills, salads, fries and coffee
is **D.A.'s Restaurant**. Upstairs, the **Glacier Store and
Tearooms** has marvelous views of the Southern Alps. The
Westland Motor Inn, tel. 728, on the main street also has big
picture-window views of the mountains and serves excellent
light and casual meals. The **THC Franz Josef**, tel. 719, has an
expensive a la carte restaurant requiring some dress-up.

Itinerary Options

At Fox Glacier, the Chalet Lookout Walk to the Cone Rock Walk
is three to four hours up and down including sightseeing time.
Within the suggested schedule, even an overnight fly-in walk-
out trip with Alpine Guides, tel. Fox 825, is possible to a hut
above the main icefall. Instead of heading for Franz Josef
tonight, another outstanding trip option is to drive (Cook Flat
Rd.) to Lake Matheson, stay overnight at the tent, caravan, bunk
or cabin facilities of nearby Fox Glacier Motor Camp, tel. 821,
or Alpine View Motel, tel. 839, for an early morning walk
around the lake and view of its justly famous reflections of Mt.
Cook and Mt. Tasman.

The Fox Glacier helihike, offered by **Alpine Guides** (tel. Fox
825) lets you ride a helicopter to the glacier and walk back
down (2 ½ hours), NZ$50 adult, including boots, socks and
parkas.

DAY 20
FRANZ JOSEF—HOKITIKA—GREYMOUTH

Spend the morning in the Franz Josef area, then head north past scenic west coast lakes, visit a greenstone factory in Hokitika, retrace the region's gold mining era and enjoy magnificent scenery before heading to Greymouth for the night.

Suggested Schedule

7:00 a.m.	Breakfast and check out.
8:00 a.m.	Franz Josef Glacier Valley Walk (or) at 9:00 a.m., the four-hour guided Franz Joseph Glacier Walk (or) flightseeing trip to Tasman Glacier.
12:00 noon	Leave for a picnic lunch and lake touring en route to Hokitika.
2:30 p.m.	Visit Hokitika's Greenstone Factory and local sightseeing.
6:00 p.m.	Dinner in Greymouth.

Orientation
The narrow strip called Westland, never more than 30 miles wide, is yet another climatically, topographically and historically unique area of New Zealand. The last ice age, ending 14,000 years ago, covered the lowland areas that now consist of dense coniferous rain forests, alpine grasslands, shrublands, herb fields, coastal lagoons and lakes and the wide gravel beds of glacier-fed rivers. Permanent ice and snow remain above 4500 feet, a bluish-white mass spilling slowly downward, cracking into deep ravines and crevasses under its enormous mass and the force of gravity, slowly retreating as 600 species of trees, shrubs, ferns and plants colonize the bare rocks in accordance with the altitude. The quantities of insects thriving on this kind of rainforest and wetland environment support comparably vast numbers and varieties of birds, which you'll hear constantly chattering and singing as you hike up to the glaciers or visit some of the beautiful lakes on the 85-mile drive to Hokitika.

The weather is relatively mild, with high rainfall south of the Westport area. Coastal growth like nikau palms and fern trees merges with coastal rain forests rising to mountain beech beneath the snow-capped peaks. The rain falls mainly at night, thereby matching Auckland for sunshine hours.

Captain Cook followed Abel Tasman on the West Coast, as he did on the North Coast of South Island. Amazingly, between

Cook's visit in 1770 and 87 years later, the West Coast wasn't approached by sea despite the hardship that Thomas Brunner and other explorers experienced on overland routes. This exploration from the Nelson area in the 1840s sought sheep and cattle country, but the discovery of gold in 1859 between Greymouth, the largest Maori settlement along the coast, and Hokitika opened a new era of settlement. Gold lured over 10,000 miners to the West Coast in the next five years including an "invasion" of Australian gold seekers. Hokitika was founded in 1864, becoming the "Capital of the Goldfields" with a hundred hotels springing up, mostly on Revell Street. The Arthur's Pass route, discovered by Sir Arthur Dobson, was opened as a coach road in 1866, when the population of the coast surged to 50,000. Greymouth and other harbors were jammed by ships bringing new miners and supplying prospectors and storekeepers. Logging and milling of local timber and the export of bituminous coal began at the same time. Coal export, centered around Westport to this day, expanded slowly for lack of port facilities and a railhead, and then grew rapidly after 1880 as gold mining declined in importance. The decline of gold mining left a string of deserted former boom towns—Charlestown, Barrytown, Denniston, Stockton and others. Shantytown, a historical reconstruction of a local gold settlement of the 1880s, is Greymouth's most popular attraction.

Sightseeing Highlights

▲▲▲Franz Josef Glacier Valley Walk takes you by minibus to the glacier and then on a glacier walk (2 ½ hours). As an alternative to the drive up the glacier there is a walking track of less than two miles on the north side of the Waiho River, going along the Callery River Gorge. At the suspension bridge where the track crosses to Glacier Road, a second track branches off to Roberts Point above the glacier. Sentinel Rock and Peters Pool on Glacier road are other easily accessible vantage points, as is Canavans Knob, which begins about a mile to the south off Highway 6.

The guided **Franz Josef Glacier Walk**, offered by the THC Franz Josef Hotel, departs at 9:30 a.m. and 2:00 p.m. for a four-hour tour. Be at the hotel at 9:00 a.m. to get your special boots, socks and orientation. Experienced guides will lead you up and down icy pinnacles and over crevasses, for an unforgettable experience costing only NZ$13 adult, NZ$7 child, including all equipment. Take a snack lunch along for nourishment while on the glacier.

▲▲▲Franz Josef to Tasman Glacier flights are offered on ski-plane or helicopter by a number of companies based in

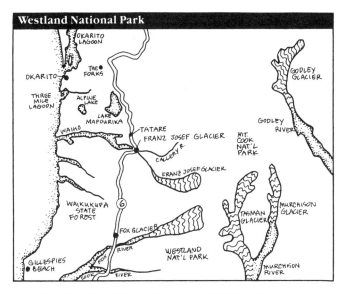

Westland National Park

Franz Josef and Fox Glacier. The cost is NZ$40-$90 per person for a ten- to 35-minute helicopter flight with Glacier Helicopters (tel. 755) or The Helicopter Line (tel. 767). For NZ$60 you can land on the snow in a 20-minute excursion with these companies or Mt. Cook Line (tel. 714).

▲▲**Hokitika**'s claim to fame started with the discovery of gold in 1864. Within two years the area had 50,000 people digging for gold and more than 100 hotels. The West Coast Historical Museum on lower Tancred Street recalls the goldmining era. Today, in addition to timber milling, several factories in Hokitika cut and polish greenstone (nephrite jade) from neighboring mountains into jewelry. Greenstone is the Maori's sacred gemstone, for which they made perilous journeys across the alps from the north and south. The Greenstone Factory, tel. 713, offers tours of the cutting and jewelry-making process on weekdays. Buy a souvenir rock or beautiful jewelry.

For magnificent local viewpoints, drive to the Plane Table Lookout north of Hokitika and the Sea View Lookout in a cemetery near the hospital. For a very picturesque view of the river mouth, walk down to Gibson Quay.

Take Blue Spur Road east of town to see the Vintage Farm Museum and Greenstone Factory, then visit the mine tunnels of the working Blue Spur Gold Mine. About 12 miles south of Hokitika, the Lake Kaniere Scenic Reserve offers a scenic drive and walks second to none.

Where to Stay

There are plenty of reasonable accommodation choices in Greymouth. The well-equipped **Kainga-ra YHA Hostel**, Cowper St., tel. 4951, at the south end of Greymouth has pleasant surroundings and costs the usual NZ$10. **Greymouth Seaside Motor Camp**, Chesterfield St., tel 6618, next to the beach, can cover most of your budget needs with tent sites, caravan sites, cabins for NZ$16 double and flats for about NZ$30 double.

For under NZ$25 per person, stay at **Dobson Cabins** (State Highway 7 at Dobson, tel. Dobson 701, or, if you prefer a B&B, **Golden Coast Guest House**, 10 Smith St., tel. 7839, or **West Haven Tourist Lodge**, 62 Albert St., tel. 5605.

The **Ace Tourist Motel**, Omoto Rd., tel. 6884, and the **South Beach Motel**, 318 Main South Rd., tel. 26-768, are NZ$45 double. **The Kings' Motor Hotel**, 44 Mawhera Quay, tel. 5085, with a restaurant, bar and pool, is up a few notches in quality and price at NZ$60 double.

Where to Eat

The best choices for light, tasty and inexpensive meals in Greymouth are **Raceway Carvery**, Union Hotel on Herbert St., tel. 4013; the cozy **Albion Bistro** in the Kings' Motor Hotel; and the **J.B. Restaurant** in the DG Greymouth Hotel, 68 High St., tel. 4361. For big barking appetites, the international menu and portions at the **West Inn**, Paroa, tel. 732, should remedy the problem.

DAY 21
GREYMOUTH—ARTHUR'S PASS NATIONAL PARK—CHRISTCHURCH

Begin the day by visiting Shantytown, an excellent reconstruction of a gold-mining town. Then start the spectacular 100-mile trip on Arthur's Pass Road (Highway 73). Crossing the Divide affords magnificent views and opportunities to explore Arthur's Pass National Park on the way back to Christchurch. Make steep ascents and descents along the twisting pathways of four glacier-fed rivers—Taramakau, Otira, Bealey and the Waimakariri—rushing through totally contrasting landscapes of mountains and foothills on the wet western and dry eastern sides of the highest highway across the Southern Alps. Scenic lookouts and both short and longer walking or hiking trails are easily accessible from the highway.

Suggested Schedule

7:00 a.m.	Breakfast and check out.
8:30 a.m.	Visit Shantytown.
9:30 a.m.	Arthur's Pass Road up to the Pass.
12:00 noon	Picnic or other lunch near Arthur's Pass Village.
1:00 p.m.	Scenic walks in the vicinity of the Village.
4:00 p.m.	Descend to Christchurch.
7:00 p.m.	Dinner in Christchurch.

Sightseeing Highlights
▲▲**Shantytown** is a faithful reconstruction of the old West Coast gold mining town, complete with hotel, church, shops, jail and gallows, livery stables, steam engine, gem and mineral hall and working gold claim where visitors can pan. Open 8:30 a.m. to 5:00 p.m.

▲▲▲**Arthur's Pass National Park** is reached from the old gold-mining town of Kumara in Westland, at the junction of Highways 6 and 73. Highway 73 traverses the Main Divide to Springfield on the western outskirts of Christchurch. As you drive along this paved and well-maintained road, try to imagine a thousand workers with picks and shovels building first the road and then the railroad over Arthur's Pass in the middle of winter; Cobb & Co. stage coaches madly racing for 36 hours to reach visions of fortunes to be made in Westland's newly discovered gold fields; and Maori using this route, without a road, to obtain precious greenstone in the river beds of the western mountains. Ascend steeply through lush grassland in the Taramakau River Valley, past the old railway town of Otira, and then cross the Otira River to Arthur's Pass. (Between Otira and Arthur's Pass caravans and trailers are banned. The alternative for returning to Christchurch is Lewis Pass.) The road is surrounded by rugged snow-capped mountains with dense beech forests to the snowlines and deep glacially-carved gorges. Follow Bealey Valley and the Bealey River into the township of Arthur's Pass. The few miles before the village, Top of the Pass, is well worth walking to get the most out of the great mountain scenery.

Allow four hours for driving from Greymouth to Christchurch and the rest of the day for sightseeing activities. Stop by the Park Visitor Centre, open seven days 8:00 a.m. to 5:00 p.m. (tel. Arthur's Pass 500) in Arthur's Pass village for information, brochures, detailed maps and to see a variety of fascinating exhibits on the history, flora and fauna, geology and other background including an audiovisual on the building of Highway 73. Just a short walk from the Visitor Centre is the Devils Punchbowl Trail to the nearby Devils Punchbowl waterfall pouring down a 400-foot gorge. The Bridal Veil Nature Walk to a view of Bealey Valley from the Bridal Veil Lookout, about an hour round trip, starts near the Bealey footbridge. Another one-hour walk from the Village, starting opposite the Dobson Memorial, winds through flower beds along Dobson Nature Walk.

From Arthur's Pass to Bealey, follow the mighty Waimakariri River within Arthur's Pass National Park. Watch for clearly signposted walking tracks, picnic shelters and camping sites. The Waimakariri River and parallel Highway 73 curve around the northern end of the tree-covered Craigieburn Range which becomes bare, eroded hills around trout-filled Lakes Grasmere and Pearson; changing again to the beech-covered Craigieburn Forest Park; and yet again from smooth round hills near Castle to a rather desolate descent from the 3000-foot level around Porters Pass to the fertile Canterbury Plains.

Itinerary Options

Returning to Christchurch, you have a choice between Arthur's Pass (Highway 73) and Lewis Pass (Highway 7). The west side of Arthur's Pass is especially lush and beautiful. The Lewis Pass Road does not offer the scenic grandeur of Arthur's Pass National Park but does open up worthwhile sidetrips—to Hamner Springs, for example. Just west of Lewis Pass is Maruia Springs, hot pools in an alpine setting. In mid-winter, Lewis Pass may be easier to cross than Arthur's Pass.

For those returning to the North Island on the Inter-Island Ferry, it's a four-hour drive from Westport to Picton, passing through the very scenic Lower Buller Gorge on Highway 6. This route opens up these options:

Coaltown Trust Museum displays the history of Westport, the country's main coal shipping port.

The Pancake Rocks and Punakaiki Blowholes at Punakaiki Scenic Reserve jut into the sea midway between Westport and Greymouth, stratified rock formations in lush greenery interlaced with rocky grottoes and blow holes.

Consider a sidetrip to the Abel Tasman National Park or the Nelson Lakes National Park.

For those wanting to stay overnight, the **Sir Arthur Dudley Dobson Memorial Youth Hostel** in Arthur's Pass Village (tel. AHP 528) has dorm beds at NZ$8 per person, and the **Alpine Motel** (tel. AHP 583) on the highway has units from NZ$30 double. The **Store and Tearooms** and the **Chalet Restaurant** in the village can take care of your lunch needs.

DAY 22
CHRISTCHURCH-BANKS PENINSULA

Take an all-day trip to the unique Banks Peninsula and Akaroa, a charming village with French atmosphere. Afterwards, return to Christchurch to relax and enjoy a special evening.

Suggested Schedule	
7:00 a.m.	Leisurely breakfast.
8:30 a.m.	Leave for all-day trip to Banks Peninsula and Akaroa.
2:00 p.m.	Visit Okains Bay.
4:30 p.m.	Drop off your car if you have an early morning flight.
	Return to Christchurch for a celebration dinner.

Driving to Akaroa
There are two ways to Banks Peninsula from Christchurch: to Lyttelton through the road tunnel under Port Hills, past many beaches and bays (Corsair, Governors Bay, Charteris Bay, Camp Bay and others), up and down the hills to Port Levy and Pigeon Bay; and the more usual route via Summit Road. Take Summit road for views stretching from Pegasus Bay to the Southern Alps and out across Banks Peninsula. Take the road through Sumner, climb Evans Pass across Bridle Path to the Sign of the Kiwi, where the road between Governors Bay and Christchurch crosses. Go straight ahead on Summit Road to Gebbies Pass and Evans Pass. Follow State Highway 75 to Birdlings Flat, skirt Lake Forsyth and continue through Little River over the hills to Akaroa Harbor. Return to Christchurch on the road through Taitapu and Halswell, staying on Highway 75 past the turnoff to the Pass.

If you have an early morning flight tomorrow, drop off your rental car tonight before dinner, saving time in the morning. But if you decide to drop it off in the morning, most car rental companies will drive you to the airport.

Sightseeing Highlights
▲▲▲**The Banks Peninsula** is geologically as well as geographically set apart from its Canterbury surroundings. Formed by two extinct volcanoes, the peninsula is cut deeply by narrow bays reached by steep roadsides off Highway 75. Akaroa is the closest that the French came to colonizing New

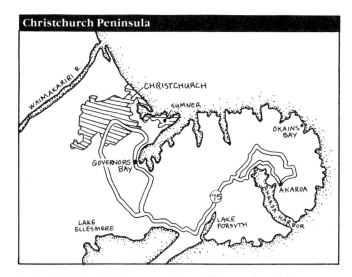

Christchurch Peninsula

Zealand. In fact, it's just an accident of history that Christ-church is very English rather than Gallic. In 1835, Jean Langlois sailed the whaling ship *Cachalot* into what today is French Bay at the site of Akaroa, sheltered from cold southerly winds. He managed to buy land from the Maoris, returned to France and organized colonists, and left France in March 1840 on the *Comte de Paris*. Britain annexed New Zealand on February 6, 1840. *Mon Dieu!* But at least Jean and the descendents of this frustrated French contingent, resting in the old French cemetery on L'Aube Hill, left their indelible imprint on Akaroa. Many street names and signs are in French. The Langlois Eteveneaux House (1845), at the rear of which is a colonial museum, has been restored by the New Zealand Historic Places Trust. A walking tour should also include visits to St. Patricks (1864) and St. Peters (1863), the domain and views from side streets on surrounding hills above the harbor.

This last day is designed for easy strolling and soaking up atmosphere in a unique, small seaside town with the appearance of a late-Victorian colonial village and a distinct get-away-from-it-all atmosphere. Just savor the relaxation after more than 1500 miles of traveling. Perhaps dangle a fishing line from the wharf, or take a launch ride in the harbor. If you want information on what to see and do in the town, stop at the Information Centre on the waterfront opposite the wharf. On the way back to Christchurch, in the same spirit visit the village of Okains Bay on the northeast side of the peninsula, just 12 miles from Akaroa. There are lovely scenic walks to explore around the bay, an unpretentious museum in a cottage, stables and a smithy with a Maori section for artifacts found on the peninsula, open daily 10:00 a.m. to 5:00 p.m. (tel. 485).

End the day soaking in a hot bath, reflecting on the trip and thinking about a superb dinner to celebrate a marvelous tour. May I recommend a suitable last dining splurge at **Grimsby's**, Montreal and Kilmore Streets, tel. 799-040, for the right atmosphere and cuisine on your final evening in New Zealand.

Depending on your choice of international carriers, the flight home tomorrow may require a change of planes or airlines in Auckland, adding about three hours to the trip back to the U.S. west coast.

PUBLICATIONS

Available at your local bookstore or directly from John Muir
Publications.

22 Days Series $6.95 each, 128 to 144 pp.

These pocket-size itinerary guidebooks are a refreshing departure from ordinary guidebooks. Each author has an in-depth
knowledge of the region covered and offers 22 tested daily
itineraries through their favorite parts of it. Included are not
only "must see" attractions but also little-known villages and
hidden "jewels" as well as valuable general information.

22 Days in Alaska by Pamela Lanier (68-0) April '88
22 Days in American Southwest by Richard Harris (88-5) April '88
22 Days in Australia by John Gottberg (75-3)
22 Days in California by Roger Rapaport (93-1) Sept. '88
22 Days in China by Gaylon Duke & Zenia Victor (72-9)
22 Days in Europe by Rick Steves (62-1)
22 Days in Germany, Austria & Switzerland by Rick Steves (66-4)
22 Days in Great Britain by Rick Steves (67-2)
22 Days in Hawaii by Arnold Schuchter (92-3) Sept. '88
22 Days in India by Anurag Mathur (87-7) April '88
22 Days in Japan by David Old (73-7)
22 Days in Mexico by Steve Rogers & Tina Rosa (64-8)
22 Days in New England by Arnold Schuchter (96-6) Sept. '88
22 Days in New Zealand by Arnold Schuchter (86-9) April '88
22 Days in Norway, Denmark & Sweden by Rick Steves (83-4)
22 Days in Pacific Northwest by Richard Harris (97-4) Oct. '88
22 Days in Spain & Portugal by Rick Steves (63-X)
22 Days in West Indies by Cyndy & Sam Morreale (74-5)

Undiscovered Islands of the Caribbean, Burl Willis $12.95   (80-X)   220 pp.

For the past decade, Burl Willis has been tracking down remote Caribbean getaways—the kind
known only to the most adventurous traveler. Here he offers complete information on 32
islands—all you'll need to know for a vacation in an as yet undiscovered Paradise.

People's Guide to Mexico, Carl Franz
$13.95   (56-7)   560 pp.

Now in its 12th printing, this classic guide shows the
traveler how to handle just about any situation that might
arise while in Mexico. ". . .the best 360-degree coverage of
traveling and short-term living in Mexico that's going." —
Whole Earth Epilog.

People's Guide to RV Camping in Mexico, Carl Franz $12.95 (91-5) 356 pp.

The sequel to *The People's Guide to Mexico,* this revised guide focuses on the special pleasures and challenges of RV travel in Mexico. An unprecedented number of Americans and Canadians have discovered the advantages of RV travel in reaching remote villages and camping comfortably on beaches. Sept '88

The On and Off the Road Cookbook, Carl Franz $8.50 (27-3) 272 pp.

Carl Franz, (*The People's Guide to Mexico)* and Lorena Havens offer a multitude of delicious alternatives to the usual campsite meals or roadside cheeseburgers. Over 120 proven recipes.

The Shopper's Guide to Mexico, Steve Rogers & Tina Rosa $9.95 (90-7) 200 pp.

The only comprehensive handbook for shopping in Mexico, this guide ferrets out little-known towns where the finest handicrafts are made and offers shopping techniques for judging quality, bargaining, and complete information on packaging, mailing and U.S. customs requirements. Sept '88

The Heart of Jerusalem, Arlynn Nellhaus $12.95 (79-6) 312 pp.

Denver Post journalist Arlynn Nellhaus draws on her vast experience in and knowledge of Jerusalem to give travelers a rare inside view and practical guide to the Golden City — from holy sites and religious observances to how to shop for toothpaste and use the telephone.

Guide to Buddhist Meditation Retreats, Don Morreale $12.95 (94-X) 312 pp.

The only comprehensive directory of Buddhist centers, this guide includes first-person narratives of individuals' retreat experiences. Invaluable for both newcomers and experienced practitioners who wish to expand their contacts within the American Buddhist Community. Sept. '88

Complete Guide to Bed & Breakfasts, Inns & Guesthouses, Pamela Lanier
$13.95 (82-6) 520 pp.

Newly revised and the most complete directory, with over 4800 listings in all 50 states, 10 Canadian provinces, Puerto Rico and the U.S. Virgin Islands. This classic provides details on reservation services and indexes identifying inns noted for antiques, decor, conference facilities and gourmet food.

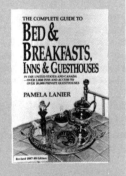

THE COMPLETE GUIDE TO
BED &
BREAKFASTS,
INNS & GUESTHOUSES
IN THE UNITED STATES AND CANADA
—OVER 2,800 INNS AND ACCESS TO
OVER 18,000 PRIVATE GUESTHOUSES
PAMELA LANIER

All-Suite Hotel Guide, Pamela Lanier
$11.95 (70-2) 312 pp.

Pamela Lanier, author of *The Complete Guide to Bed & Breakfasts, Inns & Guesthouses,* now provides the discerning traveler with a listing of over 600 all-suite hotels. Indispensable for families traveling with children or business people requiring an extra meeting room.

Elegant Small Hotels, Pamela Lanier $13.95 (77-X) 202 pp.

This lodging guide for discriminating travelers describes 168 American hotels characterized by exquisite rooms and suites and personal service par excellence. Includes small hotels in 35 states and the Caribbean with many photos in full color.

Gypsying After 40, Bob Harris $12.95 (71-0) 312 pp.

Retirees Bob and Megan Harris offer a witty and informative guide to the "gypsying" lifestyle that has enriched their lives and can enrich yours. For 10 of the last 18 years they have traveled throughout the world living out of camper vans and boats. Their message is: "Anyone can do it'!!

Mona Winks, A Guide to Enjoying the Museum of Europe, Rick Steves $12.95 (85-0) 356 pp.

Here's a guide that will save you time, shoe leather and tired muscles. It's designed for people who want to get the most out of visiting the great museums of Europe. It covers 25 museums in London, Paris, Rome, Venice, Florence, Amsterdam, Munich, Madrid and Vienna.

Europe Through The Back Door, Rick Steves $12.95 (84-2) 404 pp.

Doubleday and Literary Guild Bookclub Selection.

For people who want to enjoy Europe more and spend less money doing it. In this revised edition, Rick shares more of his well-respected insights. He also describes his favorite "back doors"—less visited destinations throughout Europe that are a wonderful addition to any European vacation.

Europe 101, Rick Steves & Gene Openshaw $11.95 (78-8) 372 pp.

The first and only jaunty history and art book for travelers makes castles, palaces and museums come alive. Both Steves and Openshaw hold degrees in European history, but their real education has come from escorting first-time visitors throughout Europe.

Asia Through The Back Door, Rick Steves & John Gottberg $11.95 (58-3) 336 pp.

In this detailed guide book are information and advice you won't find elsewhere—including how to overcome culture shock, bargain in marketplaces, observe Buddhist temple etiquette and, possibly most important of all, how to eat noodles with chopsticks!

Traveler's Guide to Asian Culture, John Gottberg $12.95 (81-8) 356 pp.

John Gottberg, *Insight Guide* editor and co-author with Rick Steves of *Asia Through the Back Door,* has written for the traveler an accurate and enjoyable guide to the history and culture of this diverse continent. Sept. '88

Guide to Bus Touring in the U.S., Stuart Warren & Douglas Block $11.95 (95-8) 256 pp.

For many people, bus touring is the ideal, relaxed and comfortable way to see America. The author has had years of experience as a bus tour conductor and writes in-depth about every aspect of bus touring to help passengers get the most pleasure for their money. Sept. '88

Road & Track's Used Car Classics edited by Peter Bohr $12.95 (69-9) 272 pp.

Road & Track contributing editor Peter Bohr has compiled this collection of the magazine's "Used Car Classic" articles, updating them to include current market information. Over 70 makes and models of American, British, Italian, West German, Swedish and Japanese enthusiast cars built between 1953 and 1979 are featured.

Automotive Repair Manuals

Each JMP automotive manual gives clear step-by-step instructions, together with illustrations that show exactly how each system in the vehicle comes apart and goes back together. They tell everything a novice or experienced mechanic needs to know to perform periodic maintenance, tune-ups, troubleshooting and repair of the brake, fuel and emission control, electrical, cooling, clutch, transmission, driveline, steering and suspension systems, and even rebuild the engine.

How To Keep Your VW Alive $17.95 (50-8) 384 pp.
How To Keep Your VW Rabbit Alive $17.95 (47-8) 440 pp.
How To Keep Your Honda Car Alive $17.95 (55-9) 272 pp.
How To Keep Your Subaru Alive $17.95 (49-4) 464 pp.
How To Keep Your Toyota Pick-Up Alive $17.95 (89-3) 400 pp. April '88
How To Keep Your Datsun/Nissan Alive $22.95 (65-6) 544 pp.
How To Keep Your Honda ATC Alive $14.95 (45-1) 236 pp.

ORDERING INFORMATION

Fill in the order blank. Be sure to add up all of the subtotals at the bottom of the order form, and give us the address whither your order will be whisked.

Postage & Handling

Your books will be sent to you via UPS (for U.S. destinations), and you will receive them in approximately 10 days from the time that we receive your order.

Include $2.75 for the first item ordered and add $.50 for each additional item to cover shipping and handling costs. UPS shipments to post office boxes take longer to arrive; if possible, please give us a street address.

For airmail within the U.S., enclose $4.00 per book for shipping and handling.

ALL FOREIGN ORDERS will be shipped surface rate. Please enclose $3.00 for the first item and $1.00 for each additional item. Please inquire for airmail rates.

Method of Payment

Your order may be paid by check, money order or credit card. We cannot be responsible for cash sent through the mail.

All payments must be in U.S. dollars drawn on a U.S. bank. Canadian postal money orders in U.S. dollars also accepted.

For VISA, Mastercard or American Express orders, use the order form or call (505) 982-4078. Books ordered on American Express cards can be shipped only to the billing address of the cardholder.

Sorry, no C.O.D.'s.

Residents of sunny New Mexico add 5.625% to the total.

Backorders

We will backorder all forthcoming and out-of-stock titles unless otherwise requested.

Address all orders and inquiries to:

JOHN MUIR PUBLICATIONS
P.O. Box 613
Santa Fe, NM 87504
(505) 982-4078

All prices subject to change without notice.